D1179958

Anti-Semitism
And the Christian Mind

Anti-Semitism
And the Christian Mind

The Crisis of Conscience After Auschwitz

Alan T. Davies

Herder and Herder

1969
HERDER AND HERDER
232 Madison Avenue, New York 10016

Library of Congress Catalog Card Number: 78–87754
© 1969 by Herder and Herder, Inc.
Manufactured in the United States

Contents

5

Foreword

Christians and Jews alike are indebted to Alan T. Davies for his perceptive and constructive analysis of the religious elements in Christian anti-semitism. If evidence be needed that genuine Judaeo-Christian dialogue can be fruitful, Dr. Davies' work provides that evidence.

Dr. Davies states with great clarity the real issue involved in creating a sound basis for relationship between the two faiths: Can the Christian's understanding of himself and his religious tradition allow for the legitimacy of the Jew's autonomous understanding of and loyalty to his own tradition? Because Judaism and Christianity are competing universalisms, to use Dr. Davies' terminology, Jews face a similar problem. They are fewer in number and less powerful. Nevertheless, normative Jewish theology tends to regard Christianity as at best a way station on the road to mankind's ultimate acceptance of God as understood by the Jewish tradition. The religious postures of both Judaism and Christianity are distinctive exemplifications of covenant theology. Both Jews and Christians are convinced that God is the ultimate actor in the historical drama, that He has entered into an exclusive relationship with an elect sector of mankind, and that there are awesome consequences involved in ignoring or rejecting His covenant. Each tradition maintains that its own institutions and beliefs are the appropriate means whereby men can enter true fellowship with God. Each is convinced that competing religious structures are at best in error if not maliciously opposed to God's plan for the redemption of mankind.

The Jewish interpretation of Christianity is perhaps somewhat more charitable than the Christian interpretation of Judaism. This may have something to do with the power relations between the two religions. Traditional Judaism maintains that Christianity is in error with regard to the special role of Jesus in the redemptive history of mankind. Nevertheless, it asserts that God requires of non-Jews only that they remain obedient to the Noahite commandments, in essence that they remain faithful to the natural law. As Dr. Davies points out, even contemporary Christian interpretations of Judaism which attempt to alleviate the burden of anti-semitism are often compelled to see the Jews as the people who, by rejecting Jesus as the Christ, rejected God's covenant and brought upon themselves their sorrowful history. Implicit in every normative Christian interpretation of Jewish experience is the conviction that Jewish misfortunes have been God's chastisement against His people for rejecting Jesus. After Auschwitz this position can only be maintained by asserting that Adolf Hitler's death camps were the instruments utilized by the just, loving and righteous God to punish His wayward people.

When I wrote *After Auschwitz,* I was convinced that the problem of God and Auschwitz presents as many theological difficulties for Christianity as it does for Judaism. Dr. Davies apparently shares that conviction. As Dr. Davies writes, it is hard to reconcile the Christian doctrine of a loving God with the death camps. At a deeper level, Auschwitz calls our attention to one of the most compelling problems faced by any religion based upon covenant and divine election. Any such religion must interpret other men's experience, values and history in the light of its own. Each version of covenant religion makes the

8

essentially imperialist claim that its way of life is better, more desirable and ultimately more in harmony with God's will than any other. In ancient times, this meant that the prophets of ancient Israel could not see much merit in the great religions of Egypt, Canaan and Babylon. Their attitude toward Canaanite religion was hostile, polemic and without a shred of appreciation of the way a great culture had come to shape the sacred dimensions of its own experience. Admittedly, there were aspects of Canaanite religion which we cannot admire such as ritual prostitution and sacrificial infanticide. Nevertheless, like the prophets we find it easier to condemn the way the Canaanites handled the problem of generational hostility and the need to celebrate fertility than to recognize how perverse are the ways in which we often deal with the same realities. Few competent anthropologists would allow that there are "inferior" or "superior" cultures. Yet implicit in all religions of covenant and divine election is precisely that conviction.

The dynamics of European imperialism cannot be divorced from those of covenant religion. Non-Europeans long ago recognized that Christian missionaries were as much an instrument of imperialism as were the armies sent forth to conquer and dominate the native populations. This was not because the missionaries conspired with the military. It was because the mentality which made it possible for the missionary to believe that he was bringing a superior culture and the true religion to "ignorant," "simple" or "uneducated" people was the pre-condition of any imperialist venture. No matter how exploitative the imperialists were, they were honestly convinced that they were "civilized" and that those whom they dominated were "savages." There were times when they did not even regard the "savages" as human beings. They insisted on understanding the experience and culture of other men exclusively in terms of their own. The way they behaved toward the non-Christians of Africa, Asia and America bears more than a little resemblance to the way Christians have reacted to Jews for two thousand years.

9

Political imperialism seems to be going out of style. In part imperialism has lost its power because non-European and non-Christian peoples no longer accept uncritically the European-Christian evaluation of their religions and cultures as in any sense "inferior" or "backward." This has in turn led to a reconsideration of the earlier European and American evaluations of non-western cultures. The twentieth century has been marked by a growing tendency of religious and national communities to understand themselves in their own terms rather than in terms defined by the once dominant European-Christian world. This is as true of the new Black self-consciousness in the United States as it is of the Vietnamese. It is increasingly true of self-respecting members of the Jewish community. Throughout the world men are in effect declaring to the Christian world:

You have an ancient and an honorable tradition. It reflects your history, your human needs and your memories. Yours is the best religion in the world for you, but not for us. We do not expect you to foresake your traditions, but we cannot accept your judgments about our culture or our sacred traditions. We will meet you only as equals. If you cannot enter into genuinely open relationship with us, it is best that our contacts remain minimal.

It is not surprising that many of the best contemporary Jewish leaders oppose any religious dialogue with Christians after Auschwitz. Their refusal must be treated with far greater seriousness than the public relations activities of Jewish defense agencies which are professionally involved in whatever "dialogue" is available to them. The values of the defense agencies are public relations values. They are often more concerned with fostering a favorable Jewish "image" than they are in risking honest, unpredictable dialogue. The Jewish religious leaders who reject dialogue speak out of the bitterness and the honesty of historical experience. They are in effect saying:

10

What is the point? You can only see all that we regard as obedience to God's will as rebellion against Him. You will not rest until
we commit the ultimate betrayal of denying our sacred traditions
and accepting yours. If there is any measure of human compassion
left in you, do not waste it on words. Leave us alone and let us
stay alive.

Such a rejection is the most predictable response to Auschwitz
as the culmination of two thousand years of anti-semitism. It
resembles the fundamental reaction since Auschwitz of those
Jews who have been free to define their existence in its own
terms without regard to Christian sensibilities. I refer, of course,
to the Jews of Israel. The creation of the State of Israel was the
fruit of many experiences, not the least of which was the massive
refusal of the survivors of Auschwitz ever again to live as a part
of Christian Europe. The survivors of the holocaust almost unan-
imously rejected day-to-day encounter, the most meaningful
form of dialogue, with their own bodies. In effect they resolved:

We may die on the sands of Palestine, but we will never again
accommodate ourselves to your good graces or your prejudices.
There may some day be another Massada in which every Jew
fights to the last man before being overwhelmed by his enemies.
There will never be another Auschwitz. Jews will never again trust
in your humanity only to endure the most degrading of impersonal
deaths. We have folded our tents. We will be wanderers no longer.
We will no longer live among you. For better or for worse, we are
going home.

At the time of the Six Day War, few Israelis were surprised
at the widespread indifference or hostility toward them apparent
among many Christian leaders. American Jews were shocked,
but not Israelis. There were also far less anger among Israelis.
Expecting little or nothing from the outside world, convinced
that in the final analysis they had only their own resources upon
which to rely, the question of Jewish-Christian relations was

11

relatively unimportant to them. In the United States, where Jews are understandably more sensitive to Christian reactions, the sense of shock was far greater. The power equation was very different. American Jews cannot ignore Christian sentiment. As a result, the meaning of the Judaeo-Christian encounter is bound to be different for Israelis and American Jews.

Discussions about religious dialogue seldom raise the issue of power. Can there be meaningful dialogue when the participants have radically different resources at their disposal? One of the reasons why dialogue between Jews and Christians has seldom been genuine is that Jews have hardly ever been able to be completely frank with Christians. Powerlessness does something psychologically and culturally to a people. It tends to inhibit their responses in such a way that open, direct communication is precluded. That is why the issues of Jewish-Christian relations cannot be focused exclusively upon the responses of Jewish and Christian leaders in the United States and Canada, but must also come to terms with the reality of Israel if it is to be meaningful. The Israelis have rejected dialogue in the most profound existential way, by removing themselves from Christian Europe. If there is to be a dialogue it must ultimately include them. They are the only Jews who are able to define themselves without reference to their status as a minority within a Christian or an Islamic society.

There is a further reason why the Israelis are important for realistic Judaeo-Christian dialogue. Many Israelis have rejected covenant theology entirely. Any attempt to regard Jews and Christians as parts of a larger biblical "household" sharing biblical faith as a common heritage must confront the Israeli reality. Israelis treasure the Bible as their most distinctive national inheritance. Nevertheless, many Israelis believe as little in the God of the Bible as contemporary Greeks believe in the Homeric gods. Israel became a reality when Jews stopped awaiting divine intervention and took their destiny into their own hands. Biblical religion is part of the heritage of every Jew;

12

however, the rejection of the Bible's fundamental perspectives about the God of history is more than a sentiment restricted to a few American radical theologians. It represents a transformation of the religious sentiments of hundreds of thousands if not millions of Jews especially in Israel. Millions of Jews no longer believe in the God of history. Jewish-Christian dialogue can no longer be based exclusively upon a common biblical faith.

It is not likely that even those Jews who seek genuine dialogue with Christians will welcome a Christian diaconate towards the Jews such as some Christian leaders propose. I believe I speak for most Jews when I suggest that even the most well-meaning expression of institutionalized *special* concern on the part of Christians for Jews will not be welcomed. Jews want neither special concern nor special malice. Many of us hope that the day may come when we will be regarded simply as ordinary men rather than as bearers of even a hint of meta-historical meaning.

Any exploration of the possibility of Judaeo-Christian dialogue after Auschwitz must face the question of individual and collective guilt. Contemporary Jews reject all attempts to make them in any way responsible for a judicial murder committed two thousand years ago in Palestine. According to Dr. Davies, many influential Christians still regard the Jews as the deicidal people. Regretably, Vatican II did not entirely settle that issue. Men who continue to regard Jews as deicides can hardly avoid interpreting Auschwitz as part of the deicidal people's just punishment. Dialogue is impossible with such men. Dialogue is only possible with men who are able to confront each other in the reality of the present. This does not mean that the past can be ignored. On the contrary, it must stand as a warning of what has happened and can happen again in Jewish-Christian relations.

Similarly, it is just as unrealistic for contemporary Christians to take upon themselves the burden of guilt for every injury ever done to Jews as it is to regard today's Jews as guilty of the

13

crucifixion. A strong Christian sense of guilt towards Jews is not helpful for either party. The dynamics of guilt are ironic. All too frequently we relieve the pressure of guilt by justifying our hostility against the victim. It is my opinion that Christians ought to be less concerned with alleviating feelings of guilt through reparative measures toward Jews or others than with the simple question: "Am I acting toward my neighbor in such a way that I can honestly respect myself?"

Christian hostility toward Jews is not likely to disappear completely. Jewish-Christian dialogue and fellowship need not await the end of hostile feelings on either side. It is, regrettably, perfectly natural that people sometimes feel hostile toward each other. If depth psychologists are correct, even the family is never exempt from death-wishes on the part of its members toward each other. If the family has its moments of extreme antagonism, is it possible that antagonism and destructive fantasies will ever be absent from group relations, especially groups so ambivalently related as Jews and Christians? It is doubtful that anti-semitic *feelings* will ever disappear. The stranger is bound to elicit both hospitality and mistrust. It is to be hoped that responsible Jews and Christians may with insight lessen the chances of the eruption of the kind of anti-Semitic *actions* which could conceivably lead to a replay of Auschwitz. We must not lose sight of the psychological reality underlying the story of Cain and Abel. Human brotherhood is an ironic, complex and precarious relationship. We are least likely to fall prey to its worst potentialities when we are capable of facing our own temptations to bring them about.

Dr. Davies deserves the sincere appreciation of both Jews and Christians for illuminating our understanding of one of the most complex and tragic forms of human brotherhood.

Richard L. Rubenstein

14

To my Mother and Father

Preface

It is unwise, I am certain, for an author to apologize at the beginning of his book under any circumstances, but there are special reasons why a study of this nature requires no apology. Few topics possess a more timely quality. Auschwitz itself, an obscure Polish village, remains a grisly monument of the not-too-distant past, at which visiting dignitaries occasionally remind themselves of Europe's most tragic moments. The Eichmann episode is still reasonably fresh in the public memory. The clamor surrounding Rolf Hochhuth's drama of a few years ago, *The Deputy,* has given birth to a continuing stream of literature concerning the enigmatic central figure of that play, Pius XII. Also not forgotten is the controversy awakened by the extension (under international pressure) of the time limit in West Germany with respect to the prosecution of war criminals. In each debate, some hint of dark passions beneath the façade of post-war western society conveyed its presence. The Arab-Israeli War in the summer of 1967 gave further indication of these passions.

As a Canadian, perhaps I may be excused if I refer in addition to the present unhappy deterioration of relations between the Jewish community in Canada, and the Christian denomination to which I belong: the United Church of Canada. This situation is largely the consequence of the anti-Israeli position adopted by *The United Church Observer* in a series of articles and editorials on the subject of the Middle East. So intense has been the resentment created among Canadian Jews by these articles that the United Church as a whole stands in danger of a generalized suspicion of anti-semitism. But not all members of that denomination support the editorial crusade against Israel sponsored by its official magazine. This book, while not written with the foregoing dispute in mind, should serve to make my own dissent clear. Indeed, I hope that the following study will assist in some measure the practical goal of improving the religious climate in Canada as far as Jews and Christians are concerned.

No apology, therefore, is necessary, except the deeper form of apology that every Christian owes to every Jew for the part which historic Christendom has played in the shaping of modern anti-semitism. Christians and Jews are involved together in whatever passions the times are stirring. Christians are involved because seldom has the church in general developed such a bad conscience about anything as it has now about the fate of the Jewish people in the twentieth century. Jews are involved because ages of humiliation and suppressed anger have now found their release in a new generation that is unafraid to defend itself against the assaults of an anti-Jewish environment. The time, consequently, is opportune for an in-depth exploration of an old disorder in Christian theology. In biblical terms, the "kairos" is ripe for a fresh encounter between Christians and Jews, in which the classical themes of guilt, repentance and reconciliation will inescapably be brought to the fore. Whatever happens, one certitude cannot be doubted: a very deep and painful moment of truth has dawned for modern Christianity.

In the following pages, post-Auschwitz Christian theology is examined from the perspective that Auschwitz provides: anti-semitism in its most extreme expression. I have attempted both a survey and a critique. As a survey, the range of material covered is as broad as possible, although necessarily selective. Some omissions are obvious. I have not tried to deal with Eastern Orthodox theology, because (except for Berdyaev) I do not know enough about it. Nor have I said much about the most conservative type of Protestant theology (except briefly in Chapter IV), because it is largely a repetition of patristic motifs without the benefit of an uneasy conscience. I may also have neglected some important Catholic and Protestant theologians. As a critique, this study is an effort not only to classify and criticize individuals, but to provide a diagnosis of the general condition of post-Auschwitz Christian thought. Whether I have succeeded or failed in this regard, others must judge.

This book was written during a year of post-doctoral research at Hebrew Union College, Cincinnati, 1967–68. To the faculty and trustees of Hebrew Union College, I am profoundly grateful for the interfaith fellowship which made this year possible. It is my hope that the result will honor both that college, where I learned a new and rich appreciation of Jewish culture and religion, and Union Theological Seminary, New York, where, as a post-graduate student, my interest in the subject was first awakened. Among individuals, I would like to express my thanks to Dr. Michael Meyer, whose seminars on Zionism and anti-semitism stimulated my own thinking; to Dr. Samuel Sandmel, who encouraged me in this project; and to Dr. Elias L. Epstein, Chairman of Hebrew Union's Committee on Graduate Studies, who was instrumental in my receiving the award.

I owe, moveover, a special debt to my former teacher, Dr. John C. Bennett, now President of Union Theological Seminary, for his sense of concern in the area of a Jewish-Christian understanding became my own concern. Indeed, although he may have forgotten the fact, this book was initially his idea.

Furthermore, I must not neglect to thank my friend, Larry

19

Martin, for having read and criticized the manuscript in its entirety. Finally, it would be inexcusably remiss of me to fail to mention the long patience of my wife, Marilyn, who accepted again the ordeals of a student existence in order that her husband's literary ambitions might come to fruition.

Grateful acknowledgment is made to the editors of the following theological journals for permission to incorporate material from articles which appeared in their pages: to *The Journal of Ecumenical Studies,* regarding my article "The Jews in an Ecumenical Context: A Critique" (Vol. 5/summer 1968/no. 3) pps. 488–506; and to *Interpretation,* regarding my article, "The Jews and the Death of Jesus: Theological Reflections" (Vol. XXIII/April, 1969/No. 2) pps. 207–217.

One word more remains to be said. The book speaks quite clearly for itself, and any mistakes are my responsibility. As a Christian, my knowledge of Judaism is more superficial than I would wish, and, while I have attempted to cite Jewish sources whenever relevant to the discussion, I am unable to claim any real competence in this field. This is, however, essentially a work in Christian theology; I trust, as a result, that some pieces of the nascent Jewish-Christian dialogue will fall into place. If this delicate enterprise is advanced by a single step, I will be fully satisfied.

Alan T. Davies

Anti-Semitism
And the Christian Mind

I. Anti-Semitism: An Inescapable Issue

Anti-semitism is not a simple topic. On the contrary, a host of problems and an imposing quantity of materials, both original and secondary, quickly belie any impressions of simplicity. First, there is the problem of definition: what exactly does the phrase "anti-semitism" mean? Different persons employ it in a variety of senses, including, in one context, everyday expressions of group prejudice, in another context the intellectual anti-Judaism of a Nietzsche, who himself disdained the "vulgar mentality" of the anti-semitic agitators of his day,[1] and, in a third context, the utter fury of Nazi *Judenhass*. While generally definable as dislike of the Jews, therefore, the fact that anti-semitism can take many forms and shapes within the range of anti-Jewish feeling renders it a difficult phrase to use consistently. Even a typing of the anti-semitic mentality in purely psychiatric terms testifies to this difficulty: "So we see that there are all shades and varieties of anti-Jewish reactions and many types of anti-Semites, ranging from the group which merely thinks in emo-

1. Nietzsche's sentiments with respect to the anti-semites of his day are expressed in various personal letters, notably the *Briefe an Mutter und Schwester*, Leipzig, 1909. Henri de Lubac uses the phrase "vulgar mentality" to describe Nietzsche's opinion of the latter in his essay, "Un Nouveau 'Front' Religieux," *Israel et la Foi Chrétienne*, Fribourg, 1942, p. 29.

23

tional stereotypes or in terms of self-interest, through the more seriously contaminated group which has fixed delusions about the Jews, to the most dangerous group of all whose hostility towards Jews is translated into overt acts of criminal violence."[2]

When we turn to history, the problem of definition becomes more acute, because the question arises as to whether all manifestations of antipathy toward the Jews from pre-Christian times until the present day should be embraced under a single label, especially when the latter has obvious nineteenth- and twentieth-century connotations. Coined in 1873 by a German pamphleteer, Wilhelm Marr,[3] the phrase "anti-semitism" was dependent on the racialist theories which were gaining momentum in France and Germany during that era. Many historians would resist the inclination to describe pre-modern periods as anti-semitic, pointing out that the phrase is only pseudo-scientific to begin with, and, in any case, could not apply to historical epochs that were innocent of modern notions of race. The force of these objections is undeniable, along with the fact that ancient and medieval anti-Judaism developed in cultural circumstances quite different from the political, social and economic forces which provided the ethos for their more recent counterpart. In a sense, anti-semitism and anti-Judaism appear disparate, and should not be confused semantically.

But is this really the case? History is a living process which cannot be divided into artificial compartments, and the past always influences the present. According to a considerable body

2. Rudolph M. Loewenstein, *Christians and Jews, A Psychoanalytic Study,* New York, 1951, pps. 24–25.
3. In Marr's pamphlet, *Der Sieg des Judentums ueber das Germanentum.*
The bad anthropology which interpreted "semite" as a racial category has long been discredited. It is probable, however, that many modern Jews possess some degree of racial connection with ancient Palestine. See C. S. Coon, "Have the Jews a Racial Identity?" and Melville Jacobs, "Jewish Blood and Culture," *Jews in a Gentile World, The Problem of Anti-Semitism,* Isacque Graeber and Steuart H. Britt (editors), New York, 1942, pps. 20–37 and 38–56.

of evidence (to be described later), earlier forms of anti-Jewish feeling entered into the mainstream of western life to find a point of contact with modern times; hence, racialist anti-semitism should not be separated too exclusively from the image of the Jew in former ages, implanted before de Gobineau, Chamberlain and Drumont ever attempted to mold popular opinion. Also, while the levels of prejudice analyzed by Loewenstein are distinct enough as individual personality types, they have intermingled with each other to comprise unified movements in society at large, so that various aristocratic establishments, military élites, political parties and segments of the general public in different times and places have developed a common anti-semitism. Despite the inexact nature of the phrase, therefore, it is probably unwise to forget that a consistent thread links the modern racialist to the very dissimilar anti-semites of the past.

A second problem, beyond the task of definition, is that of determining the cause or causes of anti-semitism. Human life, as anyone knows, has many dimensions, and can be studied from an equal number of angles: biological, sociological, psychological, historical, philosophical and theological (these do not exhaust the possibilities). The Christian has a special stake in its theological interpretation, which, of course, is not exclusive of other insights as well. Anti-semitism, as a facet of life, is susceptible to examination from all of these angles—except, I suppose, the biological—, and can be interpreted accordingly. The problem arises both within the disciplines themselves, where agreement is more the exception than the rule, and also when the attempt is made to provide a single over-arching explanation. Because of the different presuppositions involved, no one as yet has succeeded in formulating an answer that would command universal assent. Perhaps no one can.

In its most simple terms, anti-semitism is usually reduced to a species of inter-group prejudice, with, perhaps, more complicating factors than the average. A quotation from a Swedish authority may be regarded as typical: "In reality, Anti-Semitism is merely a special case of the hatred of foreigners."[4] Studies which are legion in number continue to support this view, and, for the average person, commonsense agrees. But while the truth in Valentin's statement is obvious, as far as it goes, the deeper question remains unanswered as to why the Jews have constituted a permanent "foreign" group in the various national communities (except Israel) in which their fate has been cast. Older writers, such as Bernard Lazare and Count Coudenhove-Kalergi,[5] frequently tried, sometimes superficially, to attach the whole blame to the stubborn religious particularism of Judaism, but the fact that the Nazi *Endloesung* was unleashed in the nation with the most thoroughly assimilated Jewish population in Europe is proof that ordinary xenophobia can never be more than a partial explanation. Indeed, since the Second World War and the revelation of the death camps, with their six million victims, the entire question has acquired a new perspective. After Auschwitz, conventional talk of the prejudice of a majority against a minority merely sounds hollow, and no study is adequate which does not wrestle with the heightened dimensions that the subject has now developed.

Some original and memorable insights have come from the pens of post-war writers who have gazed at man's disordered nature. In a philosophical idiom, for example, Jean-Paul Sartre describes in a famous tract the inauthenticity of people who are

4. Hugo Valentin, *Antisemitism, Historically and Critically Examined,* trans. by A. G. Chater, New York, 1936, p. 19.

5. Reflecting a characteristic nineteenth-century bias against religious orthodoxy, both of these writers urged the Jews to shake themselves free of their narrow rabbinic exclusiveness; anti-semitism, in that case, would vanish.

See Lazare, *Antisemitism, Its History and Causes,* trans., New York, 1903; and Coudenhove-Kalergi (Count Heinrich), *Anti-Semitism throughout the Ages,* edited and brought up to date by Count Richard Coudenhove-Kalergi, trans. by A. S. Rappoport, London, 1935.

26

forced to invent the Jew as a kind of convenient foil in order to avoid the threat of authentic existence. "It has become evident that no external factor can induce anti-Semitism in the anti-Semite. Anti-Semitism is a full and total choice of oneself, a comprehensive attitude that one adopts not only toward Jews but toward men in general, toward history and society; it is at one and the same time a passion and conception of the world."[6] Sartre's naïveté is exposed in his contention that anti-semitism is a bourgeois phenomenon which could not last in a communist society, because the latter is the authentic society par excellence.[7] In spite of this curious blindness, which hindsight has perhaps now dispelled, no small degree of plausibility is present in this description of human sickness in the twentieth century. Whatever else anti-semitism may be, it is beyond any question a form of human inauthenticity. Sartre does justice to the depths of the problem, but his explanation fails to cover its historical facets. For all his brilliance, he is a one-dimensional critic.

In the context of modern psychiatry, by way of contrast, Rudolph Loewenstein (whom we cited earlier) interprets anti-semitism as the product of a guilty need on the part of Christians for a "scapegoat." Basing his thesis on the results of psychoanalytic case studies of Christian patients over a period of years, he discovers that the latter show a marked tendency, because of the association of the Jews with the death of Christ, to project their own "secret sin" vis-à-vis the crucifixion—rejoicing in its occurrence—on those whom they have been taught to regard as his earthly enemies. "Thus it would seem that the basic reason, and the most ancient one, for the Jew's role of scapegoat—and in extension, of usurer, alien, inner enemy—is his participation in the death of Christ and hence in the birth of Christianity. . . . Psychologically speaking, Christians, who benefit by his death, must un-

6. Jean-Paul Sartre, *Anti-Semite and Jew,* trans. by George J. Becker, London and New York, 1948, p. 17.
7. *Ibid.*, pps. 150–151.

27

consciously rejoice in it. For it is the very cornerstone of Christianity. Each individual Christian has therefore to deal in some way with the problem of his share of guilt in Christ's death . . . [One way] to lessen the burden of guilt is to throw it all on the Jews instead of sharing it jointly with them. The next step is to project onto them also the secret sin of every Christian, of unconsciously rejoicing in Christ's crucifixion."[8]

Like Sartre's Nazi, Loewenstein's Christian requires the Jew as a scapegoat for his own inauthenticity or guilt. Apart from the general merits of Loewenstein's study, clinical evidence of this kind leaves no margin for doubting that anti-semitism is closely related to pejorative Christian doctrines concerning the Jews. Other writers, as we shall see later, have made this point in greater detail and with greater passion.

In a somewhat more grandiose spirit, the father of psychoanalysis, Sigmund Freud, writing on the eve of the Second World War, adapted the scapegoat theory to the psychic history of the human race. Assuming a collective unconscious, he traced the roots of anti-semitism to the murder of the "primeval father," as reproduced in the supposed murder of Moses and the murder of Christ.[9] The fault of the Jews (in the latter death) lies less in having shared in the murder than in having refused to acknowledge their part of the guilt; thus, to Freud, the age-old accusation, "you have killed our God" (the deicide myth), is strangely vindicated. ". . . this reproach is true, if rightly interpreted. It says in reference to the history of religion: 'You won't *admit* that you murdered God' (the archetype of God, the primeval Father, and his reincarnations) . . . Not all accusations with which anti-Semitism pursues the descendents of the Jewish people are based on such good foundations."[10]

Although the historical premises on which Freud based his

8. Loewenstein, *op. cit.*, p. 181.
9. Sigmund Freud, *Moses and Monotheism*, trans. by Katharine Jones, London and New York, 1957, pps. 113–114.
10. *Ibid.*, pps. 114–115.

theories are generally regarded as unsound, his analysis is not an exercise in fancy. In a recently published book, *After Auschwitz*, Richard L. Rubenstein employs a Freudian worldview in order to psychoanalyze the spirit of Nazi Germany as manifested in the death camps.[11] This he accomplishes with unusual skill, demonstrating the terrible potency of the deicide myth in the modern western psyche, beneath the superficial veneer of civilization.

Theology also has long studied human disorder, producing its own distinctive interpretations of what gives rise to anti-semitism. Here, a different approach to the question is opened up, with different presuppositions. To some persons, theology is likely only to cloud the issue, but this does not have to be the case. Since, as A. Roy Eckardt says, "theology and psychology are alike directly concerned with questions related to the human self . . . we may suppose that the psychological interpretation of anti-Semitism will have much in harmony with a theological point of view."[12] What this means is that the insights provided by scientific observers such as Loewenstein and Freud, or existentialist philosophers such as Sartre, are capable of further explication in the context of a Christian and biblical understanding of man. Hence, for Reinhold Niebuhr, the concept of sin, as the theological counterpart of the psychological concept of guilt, has proved a powerful conceptual means of setting the strange impulse to hate the Jews in a theological perspective, especially when sin is seen as idolatry. Anti-semitism, in this analysis, becomes a particularly virulent species of group idolatry, dedicated to the principle of preserving and exalting one's own community, that is, Christendom, at the cost of every other value.[13] Paul

11. Richard L. Rubenstein, "Religion and the Origins of the Death Camps: A Psychoanalytic Interpretation," *After Auschwitz, Radical Theology and Contemporary Judaism,* Indianapolis, 1966, pps. 1–44.
12. A. Roy Eckardt, *Christianity and the Children of Israel,* New York, 1948, p. 14.
13. Reinhold Niebuhr, "The Relations of Christians and Jews in Western Civilization," *Pious and Secular America,* New York, 1958, pps. 87f.

Tillich has also written a compelling interpretation of anti-semitism in similar theological terms, as the endless struggle of the gods of space, personified in national and racial idolatries, against the "Lord of time."[14]

Once the inquiry is extended beyond the problem of human sin, however, it quickly becomes apparent that contemporary theologians, Jewish as well as Christian, are in a state of division with respect to anti-semitism and its real depth cause. Does anti-semitism possess a metaphysical character? Is it rooted, for example, in the supernatural identity of the Jew himself as the living embodiment of Israel's election? Or are metaphysical explanations to be rejected, making anti-semitism nothing more than an ordinary spiritual problem, rooted in specific social configurations, that moral insight, if given a chance, can neutralize? This type of conflict, peculiar to religious thinkers, emerges repeatedly in theological literature touching upon the Jews today.

A parallel conflict, only more general in nature, lies between what might be described as the historical and anti-historical schools of thought. As some theologians insist that anti-semitism, whatever its human promptings, has a deeper explanation in the inscrutable will of God, various secular thinkers (who are not interested in God) also insist that anti-semitism cannot be explained in terms of history alone. Psychiatrists such as Freud and Loewenstein, for example, substitute the human psyche for the divine will. But a historian, Hannah Arendt, ridicules both the "scapegoat" theory, popular among social scientists, and the theory of "eternal antisemitism," popular among theologians, as inadequate and irresponsible. "The scapegoat explanation therefore remains one of the principal attempts to escape the seriousness of antisemitism and the significance of the fact that the Jews

14. Paul Tillich, "The Meaning of Anti-Semitism," *Radical Religion* (Vol. 4/No. 1/1938), pps. 34–36; also, Tillich's essay, "The Struggle between Time and Space," *Theology of Culture,* London and New York, 1958, pps. 30–39.

were driven into the storm center of events. Equally widespread is the opposite doctrine of an 'eternal antisemitism', in which Jew-hatred is a normal and natural reaction to which history gives only more or less opportunity."[15]

Like most professional historians, Arendt is highly sceptical of theories that do not confine themselves to tangible evidence in the historical sense. Her denunciation has a polemical ring, but it must not be ignored. There is a danger, to which theologians are especially prone, of superimposing extra-historical meanings on historical events that the facts *in puris naturalibus* cannot possibly justify. The student, therefore, is warned not to trust speculative theories of anti-semitism, theological or non-theological, which either turn a blind eye toward history, or else tailor the evidence in a subtle fashion to fit their own assumptions. We shall have occasion to recall this warning in future chapters.

A growing corpus of materials dealing with every aspect of modern and pre-modern anti-semitism continues to flow today from investigators of every description in a post-Auschwitz generation. Because the present always raises questions about the past, the best of these studies reach back in time in an attempt to locate the origins of the plight in which the Jewish people have found themselves, concentrating on both its religious and non-religious sources. Here, immediately, a further issue complicates the quest. Purely in terms of history, are the former to be considered primary, or the latter? Historians such as Jules Isaac, whose seminal studies have been pivotal in post-war Christian soul-searching, have emphasized the religious sources of anti-semitism.[16] On the other hand, scholars such as Arendt, whose investigations are no less original, have emphasized the non-religious

---

15. Hannah Arendt, *The Origins of Totalitarianism,* London and New York, 1951, p. 7.
16. Jules Isaac, *Jésus et Israel,* Paris, 1959; also the shorter English version, *The Teaching of Contempt,* trans. by Helen Weaver, Toronto, 1964, along with other writings.

sources.[17] Who is right? This debate has not yet been resolved, and is likely to rage for some time to come. Probably, both Isaac and Arendt are one-sided; in particular, the latter's analysis of how the Jew became the victim of circumstances through the collapse of his role in the European system, and therefore vulnerable when history permitted the rise of totalitarianism, leaves the religious factors too much out of account. (Arendt, incidentally, has been criticized not only for this reason, but also for misinterpreting the social and political evidence as well.[18]) Most relevant for the purposes of this book is the religious background of anti-semitism; otherwise, our study would be superfluous.

Anti-semitism, in summary, is a complex subject with many problems of definition and explanation. Sufficient has been said to establish this fact. In spite of its difficulties, however, it represents an inescapable issue for Jews and Christians alike, especially in a world that has glimpsed the depths of human evil in the crematoria of Auschwitz. Anti-semitism is first of all inescapable for the Jew, because a large share of his identity has been shaped by his participation, directly or indirectly, in the collective experience of his people, past and present. No one can understand the dynamics of modern Judaism who does not grasp this reality. Without the pressures of anti-semitism, it is doubtful if the Zionist movement would have been conceived in the nineteenth century (although that was not its only motivation), or consummated with the birth of the state of Israel in the twentieth century. An early Zionist, Moshe Lilienblum, describes in vivid language his self-discovery in a diary written during an actual pogrom in the Russia of 1881. "I am glad that I have suffered. At least once in my life I have had the opportunity of feeling

17. Arendt, *op. cit.*
18. According to Arthur Hertzberg, Arendt "has exaggerated the role of the court Jews in the formation of the European nation states in the seventeenth and eighteenth centuries."
See Hertzberg, *The French Enlightenment and the Jews,* New York, 1968, p. 6.

what my ancestors felt every day of their lives. Their lives were one long terror, so why should I experience nothing of the fright they felt all their lives? I am their son, their sufferings are dear to me, and I am exalted by their glory."[19]

Such confessions, in one form or another, can be multiplied many times over. No Christian, whose experience has been free from similar sufferings, can readily understand the inner consciousness of the Jew, or what anti-semitism has done to color his outlook and actions in modern times.

Yet anti-semitism is also inescapable for the Christian. While Christians are not threatened with the same immediacy as Jews, and, tragically, have too often been the instruments of oppression themselves, yet, because anti-semitism is a peril that sooner or later overtakes the entire human community, they must eventually expect to suffer as well. Modern totalitarian regimes have taught this lesson with a brutal clarity. As Rubenstein points out, the murder of the Jews was apparently a prelude to a larger program of liquidation. "There is no more reason to doubt Hitler's promise to find greater *Lebensraum* by exterminating Slavs than his promise to exterminate the Jews."[20] In Germany, moreover, the Third Reich, which cloaked its ideological beginnings in Christian dress, finally shed this disguise and became openly what it had always been in secret: an enemy of Christianity as well as Judaism. Thus, ironically, after centuries of alienation from its Jewish roots, the church was forced to a recognition of its own intrinsic Jewishness at the hands of the oppressors of both Jews and Christians. Regrettably, in coming to this realization, some contemporary Christians have derived a false comfort from Hitler's assault against the church. Forgetting that Nazi racism, despite its anti-Christian *élan,* owed much to the Christian theological denigration of the Jews, they tend to obscure the

19. Moshe Leib Lilienblum, "The Way of Return," trans. in *The Zionist Idea,* Arthur Hertzberg (editor), New York, 1959, p. 169.
20. Rubenstein, *op. cit.,* p. 35.

real measure of Christian guilt by disassociating Christianity from the evolution of Nazi dogmas and attitudes.[21] But the church also tasted the sweet taste of pagan self-glorification.

The latter, finally, is the most compelling reason why anti-semitism poses an inescapable issue for Christians today. From its earliest foundations, the church has involved its faith and theology in anti-Judaism. So deep and subtle has been this involvement that a modern Jewish critic can with justice speak of a Christian "predicament" with respect to the Jews,[22] since, according to traditional belief, the Jewish religion lost all right to exist after the death and resurrection of Jesus. Even today, this age-old credo has by no means breathed its last in Christian circles. During an era in which the church must reckon with a myriad of moral and spiritual convulsions, the question of its relation to the Jewish people, as part of an internal and external war against anti-semitism, continues to press its claim to first place on the theological agenda. The degree of success with which Christian wisdom can provide a solution to the oldest issue in Christian history will almost certainly affect the degree of success that the church will meet in facing the other dilemmas now disturbing its faith in an iconoclastic and revolutionary age.

21. It seems to me that John Oesterreicher concentrates too exclusively on the neo-pagan qualities of Nazism. See Oesterreicher's pamphlet, *Auschwitz, the Christian, and the Council,* Montreal, 1965.
22. Ben Zion Bokser, *Judaism and the Christian Predicament,* New York, 1967, pps. 34f.

II. Moral Upheavals After Auschwitz

The full impact of a trauma reputedly is never felt until some length of time following the causative event, whether the psyche of an individual or the psyche of a community is affected. We are living now in the third decade since the conclusion of the Second World War, with its exposé of the Nazi murder installations by the conquering allied armies, and only in the sixties are the ramifications for the human situation of what happened in the forties becoming apparent. To borrow a famous phrase from Nietzsche, Auschwitz, as the pre-eminent symbol of Hitler's final solution of the Jewish question, signifies a radical "transvaluation of values" that neither Jews nor Christians can avoid.

In a memorable paragraph, Rubenstein compares Auschwitz to Hiroshima as a decisive and irreversible turning point in history: "Six million dead cannot simply be shoved under a rug. Something has happened to man as a result. We have passed a point of no return and things will never again be the same. Now every man, not only Germans and Jews, knows that there is a terminal logic to human aggression, the logic of extermination. The bodies which went up in smoke in the chimneys of Auschwitz were joined with the bodies which were immolated at Hiroshima and Nagasaki. There is a sickness to the human predicament today which will never be clothed."[1]

According to Rubenstein, the entire character of Jewish self-understanding has been transformed by this single traumatic experience. Jews, he states, and, by implication, non-Jews as well, can never again with integrity believe in the God who exercises providential rule over human affairs; what occurred was too monstrous to be reconciled through the usual techniques of theodicy with the existence of such a God, despite the convictions of biblical faith. After Auschwitz, to trust in providence in the traditional sense is immoral as well as impossible, since it turns God into an accomplice of Hitler, deliberately willing the slaughter of the chosen people for no other reason than the crime of being chosen: "Um deinetwillen werden wir getotet den ganzen Tag . . . for thy sake are we slaughtered every day . . . (Ps. 44:22)."[2]

The claim that the God of the Bible died with Hitler's victims in the concentration camps must not be dismissed with a cheap appeal to classical faith, in spite of its iconoclastic character, and, if true, concerns more than Jews alone. Christians also have a stake in the reality of divine providence.[3] Nevertheless, the nature of the crisis posed by Auschwitz for the church is somewhat different. It is less a religious than a moral crisis, even if religion and morality can only be distinguished in a partial and

1. Jacob Neusner and Richard L. Rubenstein, "Germany and the Jews: Two Views," *Conservative Judaism* (Vol. XVII/nos. 1–2/Fall 1962, Winter 1963), p. 46.
2. Cited as a religious justification of Jewish suffering in the minds of persons still bound to biblical ideas of God's lordship over history; the quotation emerged during Rubenstein's well-publicized interview with Dean Heinrich Grueber of the Evangelical Church of East and West Berlin.
Rubenstein, *After Auschwitz*, p. 53.
3. Ulrich Simon's attempt to write a theology of Auschwitz in terms of Golgotha is a recent Christian essay on the problem. Unfortunately, Simon's analysis is rather contrived.
See Ulrich E. Simon, *A Theology of Auschwitz*, London, 1967.

arbitrary fashion. For Christians, Auschwitz, geographically and symbolically located in the heart of Christian Europe, suggests the moral disorder of the "Christian" civilization that permitted the Nazi philosophy to grow in its midst.

As we shall see, the exact degree to which Christianity contributed to the making of Auschwitz, and the other murder factories, is a complicated question to which there is no clear answer. Yet, even assuming that direct Christian responsibility was only minimal, the moral indictment of a society that, in fact, has deep Christian roots, remains indelible. While other elements assisted in shaping the Europe which emerged out of the Dark Ages, Christianity provided the cement which held together its social, cultural and religious fabric. This explains a near-axiom generally believed, if seldom articulated, by Christians: namely, that only a society formally committed to Christian values can be truly moral, and, by definition, secure against every form of barbarism. Auschwitz shattered this complacent illusion abruptly and totally. A "Christian" society is not necessarily either a good or a safe society, and Christians would be wise to spare themselves any future self-deception. That is one of the ramifications of Auschwitz for the human situation.

In light of this new look at reality, the church, willingly or unwillingly, must listen to the accusing voices of the disillusioned. Those who refuse to read the lessons of history for themselves will not lack teachers ready to point out these lessons in bold letters. One accuser is the Jew who has personally survived the holocaust, and finds himself unable ever again to trust the good intentions of Christian neighbors. There is nothing new, of course, in Jewish suspicions of Christian behavior, since centuries of pogroms have conditioned Jews to fear the worst, and frequently their fears have been realized. At the same time, a finality is present in the words of someone such as Eliezer Berkovits that implies an absolute breakdown of trust which nothing can now remedy: "All we want of Christians is that they keep their hands off us and our children."[4]

Berkovits, admittedly, is only one Jewish voice, and perhaps not typical. To regard him as an aberration who need not be taken seriously, however, would involve a serious misreading of Jewish feeling. The logic of an age-old suspicion of Christendom only has to be pressed a little harder than most Jews wish in order to reach an attitude of almost total negation. Berkovits undoubtedly overstates his case when he traces a *direct* line from the Council of Nicaea to Auschwitz, and uncritically blames the liquidation of six million Jews on "the spiritual bankruptcy of Christian religion."[5] The Nazis, as he says, were the children of Christians, and, in this sense, the guilt of the church is considerable. But they were not Christians themselves: a distinction worth something (it is not unknown for children to repudiate their fathers). Besides, anti-semitism is not that simple. Apart from its religious ingredients, factors peculiar to political, social and economic trends in modern Europe conspired to drive the Jews into "the storm center of events" (Arendt). Still, there is sufficient truth in Berkovits' rather chilling judgment against Christianity as to make his accusation difficult to refute without appearing to veil the genuine measure of Christian guilt. The church cannot shut its ears to such accusers, even when their case is exaggerated.

Equally serious is the self-accusation within the church itself concerning the failure of Christians to act as Christians at a time when a little love might have proved thoroughly practical. Is not the religious ethic of Christianity a love-ethic, rooted in the New Testament concept of *agapé?* Why, then, did it prove so impotent in the face of evil? To be sure, the exceptions were there, as the "other Germany" of the martyrs who shared the

4. Eliezer Berkovits, "Judaism in the Post-Christian Era," *Judaism* (Vol. 15/no. 1/Winter 1966), p. 82.
5. *Ibid.,* p. 77.

death march with the Jews will forever testify. But, if no Christian could have conceived or carried out a program of mass genocide, such as the Nazis, in their religious emancipation, were willing enough to carry out, neither were the majority of German Christians prepared to risk anything on behalf of Hitler's victims. In the heated debate surrounding Rolf Hochhuth's now celebrated play, *The Deputy,* most of the disputants seem to have concentrated on the least important question. Far more significant than the mystery of Pius XII's silence is the likelihood that, if the pope had spoken, his voice would have evoked almost no response. As Guenter Lewy writes: "The Pope knew that the German Catholics were not prepared to suffer martyrdom for their Church; still less were they willing to incur the wrath of their Nazi rulers for the sake of the Jews whom their own bishops had castigated as a harmful influence in German life . . ."[6]

Whether or not Hochhuth is right in his conclusions about the character of Pius,[7] the real indictment lies in the erosion of Christian values in the life of the Church as a whole, rather than in the life of one man. Both German Christianity, to which a kind of primacy in guilt belongs, and much of non-German Christianity are included in this indictment. Had centuries of religious anti-Judaism, instilled in succeeding generations, so poisoned the conscience of the ordinary Christian as to blunt his capacity to recognize simple cruelty, even when the plain evidence of the senses cried out otherwise? The fact that the moral conscience of German Christians had not wholly expired was demonstrated in the popular outcry against Hitler's odious euthanasia program, which the Catholic episcopate found the

6. Guenter Lewy, *The Catholic Church and Nazi Germany,* London and New York, 1964, p. 304.
7. The literature on this subject continues to grow. A recent defense of Pius by a Jewish author is Pinchas E. Lapide, *The Last Three Popes and the Jews,* London, 1967.

courage to denounce.[8] In the case of the Jews, however, no similar outcry occurred, and only one man, Kurt Gerstein, attempted to stem the massacre. Why? The conclusion is inescapable that prejudice, in the form described, was too powerful for the majority to resist; thus, the normal impulses of human charity came perilously close to total suffocation. In such an atmosphere, that special form of charity designated by Christians as the love-ethic of the gospel stood virtually no chance.

In varying degrees, German Christianity, since the end of the Second World War, has sought to acknowledge its responsibility for the fate of the Jews under Hitler through a compound of cowardice and indifference. Most notable, perhaps, is the 1950 resolution of the Evangelical Church, which confessed, relatively early in the game, ". . . openly that we by failure and silence are guilty before the God of mercy, of the crime that has been committed against the Jews by men of our people."[9] (Other confessions from German sources are listed chronologically in the collection entitled *Der ungekuendigte Bund.*[10])

On the strength of such utterances, one can say, without danger of exaggeration, that the mood of contrition is most intense in German religious circles at the present time. Indeed, much of the impetus behind the current efforts of Catholic and Protestant theologians in Germany, and elsewhere, to revise the Christian theological understanding of Judaism is due to this moral reappraisal. Few of these confessions, however, have appar-

8. Lewy, *op. cit.,* pps. 263–267.
9. Cited by Goete Hedenquist, "How Far has the Church accepted its Responsibility?", *The Church and the Jewish People,* London, 1954, p. 170. Hannah Arendt, incidentally, makes the interesting observation that this confession is inappropriately worded; instead of being addressed to the God of "mercy," it would be better addressed to the God of "justice," since justice rather than mercy has been outraged in the murder of six million Jews obviously innocent of any crime!
See Hannah Arendt, *Eichmann in Jerusalem, A Report on the Banality of Evil,* London and New York, 1965, p. 296.
10. *Der ungekuendigte Bund, Neue Begegnung von Juden und christlicher Gemeinde,* Stuttgart, 1962, pps. 248–272.

ently convinced Jews that Christians are really in a state of repentance deep enough to rule out the possibility of future silences of the same kind. Nowhere has this mistrust become more evident than in the reaction of Jews (and some Christians) to the well-publicized 1965 Vatican schema, *Declaration on the Relation of the Church to Non-Christian Religions,* which was the final product of a bitter and prolonged internal struggle behind the scenes of the four sessions of the recent Ecumenical Council.[11] Of necessity, this schema was a compromise, and, like most compromises, successful in pleasing almost no one. In fact, not many documents have the distinction of combining the qualities of success and failure so markedly at the same time.

The schema has been both praised extravagantly and denounced harshly. It has been praised by liberal Jewish voices who have seen in its promulgation the ending of a long heritage of ecclesiastical anti-Judaism, and the promise of a new dawn in Jewish-Christian relations. Thus, for example, Joseph L. Lichten was able to write, "That historic Thursday (Oct. 28th, 1965) left many of us with a feeling, above all, of relief that the fundamental ground for disharmony between the two communities had been swept clear. . . ,"[12] and Samuel Sandmel, moved by the idea of a Christian declaration on the Jews, has composed his own Jewish declaration on the Christians, absolving the latter from responsibility for the anti-Jewish attitudes and deeds of their ancestors.[13]

But such voices were not the only voices. Once again, the dissenters have not been slow to speak. Hence, Joel Carmichael concluded that, because the Vatican Declaration fell short of a

11. For a detailed account, see Arthur Gilbert, *The Vatican Council and the Jews,* Cleveland, 1968.
12. See Lichten's essay, "The Council's Statement on the Jews," *The Star and the Cross, Essays on Jewish-Christian Relations,* Katharine T. Hargrove (editor), Milwaukee, 1966, p. 223.
13. Samuel Sandmel, *We Jews and You Christians, An Inquiry into Attitudes,* Philadelphia, 1967, p. 145.

41

genuine liberalization on the deicide issue, its value was questionable,[14] and Berkovits even doubted the possibility of sincere repentance on the part of Christians: "All the friendlier statements about Jews and Judaism made in this new age by the Church and Christianity must be comprehended in the light of the change imposed by external historic developments upon Christianity. This certainly applies to the Vatican Council's schema on the Jews. It was forced on the Church by the new historic constellation."[15]

Interestingly enough, an even more rigorous denunciation has come from a Protestant critic, A. Roy Eckardt. "If by some trick of time this schema could have been promulgated in the thirteenth century, the ideology in it would have been redeemed a little. The powerful are sometimes brought to do justice to the powerless. But in the present instance, while the voices are voices which would foster understanding, the hands are hands which have clasped death: the death of Christendom, the 'death of God', and the death of six million Jews. How admirable of us now to exonerate the Jewish people for all their reputed transgressions! Could there be a more damning judgment upon the church of our century than this one—that not until after the day of Auschwitz did Christians see fit to fabricate a correction of the record?"[16]

Both Berkovits and Eckardt, one gathers, would have preferred that such a piece of hypocrisy had never been fashioned. But is their condemnation justified?

Berkovits is probably right in claiming that the end of Christian ascendancy (the so-called "age of Constantine") has forced the church, somewhat against its own will, to reassess its situa-

14. See Carmichael's review of Xavier Rynne's book, *The Third Session*, in *Judaism* (Vol. 14/no. 3/1965), pps. 380–382.
15. Berkovits, *op. cit.* p. 76.
16. Eckardt, "Can There Be a Jewish-Christian Relationship?", *The Journal of Bible and Religion* (Vol. XXXIII/April 1965/no. 2), p. 124.

tion in the world. In part, "aggiornamento" was less the inspiration of a single charismatic personality, Pope John XXIII, than the result of factors which ultimately left the papacy only the alternatives of reform or ossification. For this reason, the schema was not so much a spontaneous act of reform as a calculated reckoning with a radically altered state of affairs, in which, after sixteen centuries, Christians have been thrust from the protective shelter of the *societas Christiana* into an encounter on equal terms with the Jews and the other great religious communities of mankind. This aspect of *Realpolitik,* however, does not preclude a sincere conscience on the part of its originators. Although Cardinal Bea and his secretariat may have been unsuccessful in transmitting the true depth of their concern into the actual text, the former's speech before the Council, delivered as an apologia for such a proclamation concerning Judaism, leaves no doubt as to the inner travail of his mind.[17] Nonetheless, the absence in the final draft of any suggestion of Christian complicity in anti-semitism remains a grave deficiency; here, criticism is legitimate.

Because the self-accusation of someone who feels guilty is, in a sense, more consuming than the moral indignation of someone who feels wronged, it is Eckardt, the Christian, rather than Berk-

17. Augustin Cardinal Bea, "Catholics and Jews," *Council Speeches of Vatican II,* ed. by Hans Küng, Yves Congar, Daniel O' Hanlon, Glen Rock, 1964, pps. 258–259.

"But why is it so necessary precisely today to recall these things? The reason is this. Some decades ago anti-Semitism . . . was prevalent in various regions and in a particularly violent and criminal form, especially in Germany under the rule of National Socialism, which through hatred for the Jews committed frightful crimes, extirpating several millions of Jewish people. . . . Moreover, accompanying and assisting this whole activity was a most powerful and effective 'propaganda' . . . against the Jews. Now it would have been almost impossible if some of the claims of that propaganda did not have an unfortunate effect even on the faithful Catholics, the more so since the arguments advanced by that propaganda often enough bore the appearance of truth, especially when they were drawn from the New Testament and from the history of the Church. Thus, since the Church in this Council is striving to renew itself by 'seeking again the outlines of its most fervent youth' . . . it seems imperative to take up this question."

ovits, the Jew, who reveals an emotional loss of objectivity in his attack on the Vatican Declaration. (Eckardt, it must be said, is a theologian of importance in the complex realm of Jewish-Christian relations, as well as—like James Parkes[18]—a prophetic voice in the Christian world who has not, at times, been afraid to stand alone. His theology will be described later. For the moment, his inability to see any merit in the schema must occupy our attention.) Surely Eckardt has neglected the obvious point that, however condescending it may sound, the exoneration of the Jewish people "for all their reputed transgressions"—an utterance addressed to Christians rather than Jews—has the pragmatic advantage of warring against exactly the kind of popular religious scorn that so effectively paralyzed the conscience of German Christianity during the Nazi era. There is no question but that the "teaching of contempt" (Isaac) would have been better denounced in the thirteenth century (in which case, the course of European history would probably have assumed a different direction), but the impossibility of altering the past does not invalidate the efforts of the present to alter the future. The true test of the schema will lie in its fruits.

Eckardt, however, is justified in speaking of an ideology insofar as one powerful motive behind recent papal attempts to engage in dialogues with the representatives of other faiths still seems to be the same old determination to bring everyone outside the church to the waters of baptism:[19] a motive resented by most non-Catholics, but especially resented by Jews, who have suffered severely from conversionist tactics on the part of militant bishops in the past. But almost nothing is free from some ideological taint, and, in this case, the motive of conversion was

18. See Chapter III.
19. Expressed, for example, by Paul VI in his comments concerning the "separated brethren" at the opening of the Second Session, September 19, 1963. See Xavier Rynne, *The Second Session, The Debates and Decrees of Vatican Council II, September 19–December 4, 1963,* New York, 1963, pps. 357–358.

sufficiently repressed by the authors of the schema so as not to obscure its more important emphasis on the solidarity of Jews and Christians in a common "spiritual patrimony."[20] To speak of the Vatican declaration as a fabrication means more than calling to task the intrinsic phoniness of one ecclesiastical document. It implies that, after Auschwitz, the only possible thing for the church to do is to keep silent, since any Christian attempt to amend the record will merely serve to intensify the damning judgment of history, like a bad apology after an inexcusable lapse of decent behavior. Perhaps Eckardt has a point in this criticism, but perhaps also it is better to risk the bad apology rather than risk a replay of the terrible drama that an uncorrected record might help to prompt.

Yet the declaration is far from being an adequate, much less a perfect statement; the accusing voices of the Jews and Christian critics give that fact a painful clarity. In the first place, as its background in the Council proves, it was the product of a compromise between the conservative and progressive factions;[21] and while their power struggle made a truncated schema inevitable, no compromise ever does justice to the moral implications of any issue. As far as this particular issue is concerned, moreover, the matter was made immeasurably worse by a residue of anti-Jewish feeling which lingered in an undisguised form among some of the conciliar delegates themselves.[22] In the second place, the unhappy intrusion of Arab-Israeli politics into the Council, beginning with the Wardi Incident,[23] cast a shadow of expediency

20. *Declaration on the Relation of the Church to Non-Christian Religions,* article 4.

21. Prior to its final promulgation, Rynne writes, the declaration on the Jews was "treated as a kind of theological football tossed back and forth behind the scenes."

Rynne, *The Third Session, The Debates and Decrees of Vatican Council III, September 14–November 21, 1964,* New York, 1964, p. 67.

22. For example, Bishop Luigi Carli of Segni.

23. Gilbert, *op. cit.,* pps. 61f.

over the delaying and watering-down tactics to which the original draft was subjected, and this shadow has not been forgotten. The spectacle of political interference in a religious assembly with regard to a moral question is necessarily unattractive. When, however, this situation was compounded by a reluctance on the part of the delegates to include in the declaration an admission of Christian guilt, no one should be surprised if the world reacts with a measure of scepticism. Even the most sympathetic Jewish critics have spoken adversely of this defect. "Overriding all . . . was the absence in the Declaration of any note of contrition or repentance for the incredible sufferings and persecutions Jews have undergone in the Christian West. The Church's various declarations asked forgiveness from the Protestants, the Eastern Orthodox, from the Moslems, but not from the Jews. Many Jews, especially those who lived through the Nazi holocaust, asked with great passion, 'How many more millions of our brothers and sisters will need to be slaughtered before any word of contrition or repentance is heard in the seats of ancient Christian glory?'"[24]

If Marc Tanenbaum, who otherwise hails the schema, does not hesitate to utter such a sharp rebuke, why should an unsympathetic person such as Berkovits shock Christians because he sees no merit in it at all?

What has been said of the Vatican declaration can be said with equal justice of the rather tepid condemnations of antisemitism recorded by the various assemblies of the World Council of Churches: Amsterdam, 1948; Evanston, 1954; New Delhi, 1961[25] (the 1968 assembly at Uppsala apparently did not pur-

24. Marc H. Tanenbaum, "A Jewish Viewpoint," *Vatican II: An Interfaith Appraisal,* International Theological Conference, University of Notre Dame; March 20–26, 1966, ed. by John H. Miller, C.S.C., Notre Dame, 1966, p. 363.
25. For example, the following:
"The Assembly urges its member churches to do all in their power to resist every form of anti-semitism. In Christian teaching the historic events which led to the Crucifixion should not be so presented as to

sue the question). Judging from these statements, it appears that Protestants also have failed in producing the fruits of repentance in sufficient degree to overcome the Jewish suspicion of a hidden Christian anti-semitism, ready to surface at any moment in a world not so much "come-of-age" as suddenly grown old. A confession of guilt (if one is possible) that is truly convincing to the Jewish community, therefore, seems an unavoidable step if Jewish-Christian relations are to achieve the kind of breakthrough that the situation requires. There is nothing vindictive or unreasonable in the desire of Jews for such an expression of Christian self-honesty; rather, it is a matter of restoring basic trust in purely human terms. However painful its recognition may be to the Christian ego, the life of the church is at stake in this moral crisis. "A species, when no longer adapted to its actual environment, can evolve, or it can perish. The Church cannot perish. But there is a third possibility. Sometimes a species succeeds in taking refuge in a backwater of existence, where—in diminished numbers and with no further relevance except to historians of past evolution—it prolongs an insignificant story."[26]

Assuming that Christopher Butler's scientific analogy is sound, no half-hearted coming to terms with the sources of anti-Judaism in the Christian tradition will suffice to save institutional Christianity from the fate he describes, for a church unwilling to admit its sin in one sphere is bound to reflect the same spiritual recalcitrance in other spheres. The catharsis, moreover, must be deep. Anti-semitism is more than a minor evil in the catalogue of human misdemeanors; instead, it has to be classified as a major sickness of western history, with, perhaps, pathological

---

fasten upon the Jewish people of today responsibilities which belong to our corporate humanity and not to one race or community . . ."

See *The New Delhi Report*, "The Third Assembly of the World Council of Churches, 1961, New York, 1962, p. 148.

26. Abbot Christopher Butler, O.S.B., "The Aggiornamento of Vatican II," *An Interfaith Appraisal*, p. 7.

roots in the unconscious as well as the conscious mind of western man. Freud's theory has already been mentioned. Whether or not anti-semitism, as he believed, re-enacts man's primeval parricide, or (as he also believed) represents a pagan backlash against the "Jewish" God in whose name the nations were forcibly baptized,[27] it unquestionably signifies a radical disorder within the piety and theology of Christendom, causing the tree of faith to bear bad fruit. On that point, Freudians and non-Freudians agree. For this reason, the guilt of the children of western civilization is not a superficial guilt, but something that must be exposed, confessed and exorcised in its conscious and subconscious depths. Simply to condemn the manifestations of anti-semitism as a violation of "God's all-embracing love"[28] merely begs the question.

If, however, the anti-semitic impulse is discovered to lie largely beneath the surface, one temptation must be avoided. Although easily led in this path, Christians indicted by their Jewish brothers dare not plead the power of strange unconscious emotions as an excuse for a lamentable absence of charity on the conscious level of their human relationships. This raises, of course, the delicate problem of personal responsibility. Is the brainwashing of old and new varieties of anti-Jewish propaganda in the religious and intellectual ethos of a nation for a long period of time really a sufficient reason for the people (or, at least, many of them) to act like beasts? After all, we have already admitted that the conscience of German Christianity had been seriously impaired as far as the Jews were concerned. Is all responsibility, then, erased? The answer still has to be no. As long as man retains some of the attributes of his essential humanity, no matter what drives plague him beneath the surface, in purely conscious terms he has not lost control of his responses as a human being. Even if its substance is damaged, the conscience remains. The truth, therefore, is that German Christians, how-

27. Freud, *op. cit.,* p. 117.
28. *DRCNCR,* p. 7.

48

ever persuaded by the charges constantly dinned into their ears about the Jews, ought to have been capable of a more "Christian" mode of thinking and acting in the concrete situation. Were not Christian children in Germany also nurtured in the elements of Christian charity? Religious prejudice could not have been the only attitude instilled in the catechetical teaching of the church. Lutheranism, in particular, has always stressed the unique purity of *agapé* as the inward motif of the Christian life. The fact that a minority of German Christians—the martyrs—were able to live and die according to its demands, proves that many more might have done so, had they been willing to struggle against the dark image of Judaism which so tenaciously stifled their minds.

The majority, however, chose the opposite course. This hard reality has some important implications for Christian ethics. Some reconsiderations concerning the efficacy of certain Christian beliefs are in order. The most noble religious concept is revealed as powerless, if, knowing what God wills, *homo religiosus* nonetheless acts consistently otherwise. In the case of anti-semitism, the moral issue, in the last analysis, was very simple. The cry was a cry of humanity, and even a corrupted conscience should have responded. (There is no scope here for pleading that too many ambiguities stood in the way of a reliable moral decision: a plea that has occupied the mental energy of some moral theologians in the twentieth century, and which, in many instances, is certainly not lacking in validity.) What is raised, consequently, is the question of a more effective conscience, that is to say, a conscience with a more compelling basis in the Christian's self-identity. Such a conscience would be capable of something beyond a mild censorship when wrong is committed, that is, of being a "bad" conscience. Its potency would extend to right-doing in the deepest human sense of a positive moral responsibility in the world as the realm of God's loving concern, and thus the realm of man's active stewardship.

As Paul Lehmann has emphasized, the conscience is in serious trouble today. By and large, it has lost its power. In his lengthy treatment of the subject, Lehmann traces its fate in the intellectual odyssey of western man. "The semantic, philosophical and theological pilgrimage of conscience begins with the Greek tragedians of the fifth century before Christ and ends with Sigmund Freud. It is a moving, tortuous record of decline and fall which forces upon us in our time the frankest possible facing of a sharp alternative: either 'do the conscience over' or 'do the conscience in'!"[29]

Obviously, Lehmann prefers to do the conscience over. That is our choice as well; the conscience must regain its ancient numinous power. There is, however, a problem. Lehmann's hope is for a restoration of the (Christian) conscience within the context of the church (or *koinonia*) as its necessary environment, since faith alone can breed the motivation and provide the content for ethical living in a Christian sense. In principle, this view is probably sound, but a danger lies in forgetting the difference between the ideal church and the real church. As we have seen, the church as a whole can suffer corruption just as surely as the individual Christian. It was precisely in this "context" that the abdication of moral obedience as far as Christian charity was concerned was most evident and most heinous. If the religious community is to be the context for a restored Christian conscience, then it would seem that the community must be nursed to health first. This conclusion returns us to the unsettled matter of an adequate confession of guilt for Christian complicity in the destruction of Europe's Jews under Hitler. Only through such a confession—a confession unafraid to feel the pain of Christian guilt with the classical remorse of an Orestes, when conscience entailed inner terror and agony—is the church likely to experience the measure of healing that would make it a suitable catalyst for breathing new power into the

29. Paul Lehmann, *Ethics in a Christian Context,* New York, 1963, p. 327.

consciences of its members. In the absence of this collective healing, it is more difficult for individual Christians, on their own initiative, to undergo the catharsis required if the conscience is to mean anything vital in an age innately suspicious of concepts with religious dimensions.

The moral upheavals that Auschwitz has stirred in the world of conventional religion and traditional morality are only beginning to make their real impact felt. The crisis that faces Christianity is essentially a moral crisis much more serious than is generally believed. It is a crisis of conscience that, in the end, raises questions concerning the nature of the conscience itself. For this reason, anyone who thinks that the churches have uttered their final word on the subject of anti-semitism, so that the matter may now be swept safely under a rug and conveniently forgotten, surely cannot read the signs of the times.

III The Case For and Against Christianity

To what extent is Christianity actually responsible for the rising spiral of modern anti-semitism which culminated in Auschwitz? This question, which is difficult to answer with exactitude, is being debated by Jewish and Christian scholars both. One point, however, is indisputable: the church is not innocent. No washing of Christian hands can establish such a verdict. The mere fact that the church served as the caretaker of western society for almost sixteen centuries is sufficient proof of at least an indirect guilt, since anti-semitism developed on soil well watered by Christian ideas. Our question, then, is really a question of degree, and here, as elsewhere, no unanimity of opinion exists.

Few Christians, even those moved to a confession of "failure and silence" in the face of Hitlerism, were prepared for the massive indictment which some critics (such as Berkovits) have directed against so much of their tradition. It has been a shock —almost as great a shock as the discovery of the death camps themselves—to be told that anti-semitism, despite its neo-pagan, racialist dress, owes its true origins to Christian teachings. In one sense, of course, this indictment is not novel, as many Jews intuitively associated anti-semitism with Christianity much earlier than Auschwitz, but until Auschwitz gave the matter a new and more terrible urgency, few Christians had taken the charge seriously. To understand the present encounter between Jew and Christian, it is necessary to contend with the case against Christianity in its most unqualified terms.

The charge that Christian religious prejudice is the real reason for the precarious existence of Judaism in the twentieth century has not only been made by Jews. At least one non-Jewish observer of the historical scene, the Anglican scholar James Parkes, has uttered the same accusation. Like Arendt, Parkes recognizes that anti-semitism is partly the creation of secular history, and not the product of religion alone.[1] "With a suitable rechauffée of all the previous fables, the immense structure of modern antisemitism was reared."[2] But the basic ingredient in the "drama of artificiality," he believes, is the theological portrait of the Jew drawn by the church fathers in the third and fourth centuries: a portrait that provided the foundation for the variations and embellishments of later ages. "The Jew as he is encountered in the pages of fourth-century writers is not a human being at all. He is a 'monster', a theological abstraction, of superhuman cunning and malice, and more than superhuman blindness. . . . The Fathers obtained the perspective of a distorting mirror and drew faithfully what they saw. The monstrosity of Israel was evident to them. There was not one single virtuous action in her history. She had been a perpetual disappointment to God, in spite of all the wonderful things He had done for her."[3] In short, patristic theology is the villain of the piece.

The same charge, arising from the grievance of personal tragedy, is made by the French Jewish historian, Jules Isaac. To Isaac, Christian anti-semitism has been "the powerful trunk,

1. James Parkes, *An Enemy of the People: Anti-Semitism,* New York, 1946, pps. 63–66.
2. *Ibid.,* pps. 65–66.
3. James Parkes, *The Conflict of the Church and the Synagogue, A study in the origins of antisemitism,* London, 1935, pps. 158–159.

with deep and multiple roots, upon which have been grafted other varieties of anti-Semitism, even varieties as anti-Christian as Nazi racialism."[4] Once again, the theological literature of the patristic age is blamed for creating a "teaching of contempt"[5] in ecclesiastical tradition which has infected each generation of Christians since early times. "But if one reflects, as we must reflect, that such teaching has been disseminated from generation to generation, by hundreds and thousands of voices, often the most eloquent, often also the most grossly insulting voices, how can one be surprised that the Christian mentality is encrusted with it, modelled upon and fashioned by it, even to the depths of its subconscious; and that, little by little, especially in the fourteenth and fifteenth centuries there should be formed in Christendom a picture of Judaism and Jews which is both a caricature and a myth; an ignoble image, engendering repulsion and hate?"[6]

When one examines the actual writings of the period under attack, it is difficult not to be convinced that Parkes and Isaac are right. Theologically, Judaism fares extremely badly. As early as the second century, the process of depriving the Jews of their place in "salvation history" (or "*Heilsgeschichte,*" to use von Hofmann's well-worn theological phrase) had begun. In the *Epistle of Barnabas,* for example, the church is exalted at the expense of the synagogue, which, like Manasseh, is now the discredited older brother.[7] Similarly, in Justin Martyr's *Dialogue with Trypho,* Christians are featured as the "true Israelitic race"

4. Jules Isaac, *Has Anti-Semitism Roots in Christianity?* trans. by Dorothy and James Parkes, National Conference of Christians and Jews, New York, 1961, pps. 55–56.

5. Isaac, *The Teaching of Contempt, Christian Roots of Anti-Semitism,* trans. by Helen Weaver, New York, 1965.

6. Isaac, *Has Anti-Semitism Roots in Christianity?* p. 61.

7. Chapter XIII, *The Epistle of Barnabas,* trans. in *The Ante-Nicene Fathers,* Alexander Roberts and James Donaldson (editors), American reprint of Edinburgh Edition, Grand Rapids, 1950, Vol. I, pps. 145–146.

and Jews are reduced to the lowly status of Jacob's biological offspring whom God "reproached with unfitness for the inheritance."[8] To Justin, the mildest of the early fathers, Israel "begotten by flesh and blood" had offended God by spurning the messiahship of Jesus, for "he who insults and hates Him [Christ], insults and hates Him [God] that sent Him."[9] Only if the Jews repent and accept the Lord whom in the "highest pitch of [their] wickedness" they had slain, is there any hope.[10] Thus, in Justin's era, the notion of deicide with its ominous overtones started to appear in Christian literature. Later theologians took up this theme with alacrity.

The third-century apologist, Tertullian, lends stronger support to the case against Christianity. Tertullian, whose mind had a legalistic bent, argued in his polemic *Contra Judaeos* that, because the messiah's coming would be accompanied by divine judgment on Israel, the Jews, having already in 70 A.D. suffered political and military catastrophe at Roman hands, possessed no excuse for not believing in Jesus. "Since, therefore, the Jews were predicted as destined to suffer these calamities on Christ's account, and we find that they have suffered them, and see them sent into dispersion and abiding in it, manifest it is that it is on Christ's account that these things have befallen the Jews, the sense of the Scriptures harmonizing with the issue of events and of the order of the times. . . . Restore to Judaea the condition which Christ is to find, and [then, if you will] contend that some other [Christ] is coming."[11]

This mode of proving the spiritual destitution of Judaism from history (which, incidentally, has New Testament antecedents) became a much employed argument in traditional

8. Chapter CXXXV, Justin Martyr, *Dialogue with Trypho*, trans. in *The Ante-Nicene Fathers*, Vol. I, p. 267.
9. *Ibid.*, p. 268.
10. *Ibid.*
11. Tertullian, *Contra Judaeos*, trans. in *Ante-Nicene Christian Library*, Edinburgh, 1870, Vol. XVIII, p. 253.

apologetics: indeed, a patristic commonplace which, as we shall see later, still casts a spell over Christian thinking. Tertullian, significantly, was so ignorant of Jewish religious concepts that he regarded circumcision as a divine plot for identifying Jews in order that Roman officials might prevent the latter from entering the city limits of Jerusalem during the apologist's own lifetime![12] The greater the ignorance, the deeper the hostility tended to grow.

Worse again was Hippolytus. To this author properly belongs much of the inspiration for the theme of malediction: that is, the idea that the Jews, like Cain, existed under God's curse. In his exposition of the sixty-ninth Psalm, Hippolytus used the occasion to enlarge on the perpetual servitude earned by the Jewish people for their cruel treatment of Christ: "Listen with understanding, O Jew, to what the Christ says: 'They gave me gall for my meat; and in my thirst they gave me vinegar to drink.' And these things He did indeed endure from you. Hear the Holy Ghost tell you also what return He made to you for that little portion of vinegar. For the prophet says, as in the person of God, 'Let their table become a snare and retribution.' Of what retribution does He speak? Manifestly, of the misery which has now got hold of thee . . . Furthermore, hear this yet more serious word: 'And their back do thou bend always'; that means, in order that they may be slaves to the nations, not four hundred and thirty years as in Egypt, nor seventy as in Babylon, but bend them to servitude, he says, 'always'."[13]

The same predilection for twisting history in light of a prejudiced theology emerges in Cyprian, whose collection of scriptural testimonies provided the most concise epitome of early Christian beliefs concerning the Jews. In his letter to Quirinus, the African

12. *Ibid.,* p. 208. Parkes regards this statement as "bitter sarcasm" on Tertullian's part (*CCS,* p. 104); probably, however, Tertullian intended it literally.

13. Hippolytus, *Expository Treatise against the Jews,* trans. in *The Ante-Nicene Fathers,* Vol. V, p. 220.

bishop summed up the subject under twenty-four headings, in the course of which he appropriated all the blessings of Hebrew prophecy for the church, leaving only the curses for the synagogue. An example is the following: "In Isaiah: 'Your country is desolate, your cities are burned with fire: your land, strangers shall devour it in your sight; and the daughter of Zion shall be left deserted, and overthrown by foreign peoples'."[14] Like Tertullian, Cyprian connected this type of prophetic threat in the Old Testament with the much later Roman subjugation of Judaea in 70 A.D. Neither theologian, apparently, entertained for an instant the possibility of historical coincidence; both interpreted scripture with a literalistic zeal that insisted on reading every significant event in direct providential terms. As far as the Jews were concerned, no other meaning except divine wrath seemed possible to the patristic mind when the church reflected on Jewish misfortunes in recent history.

Another example of the same mentality is supplied by Eusebius of Caesarea. To this father, Christian theology owes the quaint distinction between "Hebrews" and "Jews."[15] The Hebrews included the patriarchs and prophets of the Old Testament, whom Eusebius regarded as proto-Christians; the Jews, on the other hand, included "all the evil characters."[16] This style of theologizing is important, because it represents what is probably the first ecclesiastical attempt to blacken the very name of Jew by definition. Needless to say, later anti-semetic writers capitalized greatly on phony semantic arguments of this kind.

14. Cyprian, *Ad Quirinum,* trans. in *The Ante-Nicene Fathers,* Vol. V, p. 510.
15. Eusebius of Caesarea, *Preparatio Evangelica,* Book VII, Chapter VI:
"And that you may know the difference between Hebrews and Jews thus: the latter assumed their name from Judah, from whose tribe the kingdom of Judah was long ages afterwards established, but the former from Eber, who was the forefather of Abraham."
See E. H. Gifford's translation, Oxford, 1903, p. 327.
16. James Parkes, *Judaism and Christianity,* Chicago, 1948, p. 116.

Perhaps, however, the most deadly witness against Christianity is the eloquent preacher of the eastern church, St. John Chrysostom, a charismatic prelate who could not restrain his animosity. The following selection from one of Chrysostom's homilies on John's Gospel (a sermon, incidentally, later than the notorious anti-Jewish homilies delivered in Antioch during the years 386–387) illustrates the degree to which the Christian imagination of the fourth century had become incapable of expounding scripture without distorting the most simple text in an anti-Jewish fashion. His subject is the cry of the people to release Barabbas instead of Jesus. "O accursed decision! They [the Jews] demand those like mannered with themselves, and let the guilty go; but bid him punish the innocent. For this was their custom from old time . . . Pilate scourged Him, perhaps desiring to exhaust and to soothe the fury of the Jews. For when he had not been able to deliver Him by his former measures, being anxious to stay the evil at this point, he scourged Him, and permitted to be done what was done, the robe and the crown, to be put on Him, so as to relax their anger. Wherefore also he led Him forth to them crowned, that, seeing the insult which had been done to Him, they might recover a little from their passion and vomit their venom. 'And how would the soldiers have done this, had it not been the command of their ruler?' To gratify the Jews. Since it was not by his command that they at first went in by night, but to please the Jews; they dared anything for money."[17]

One feature of this diatribe is worth special notice, namely, the subtle process whereby Pilate is ennobled as the Jews are debased. The *reductio ad absurdum* of this literary trend was achieved in the popular medieval portrayal of Pilate as a Chris-

17. *The Homilies of S. John Chrysostom, Archbishop of Constantinople, on the Gospel of John,* trans. by members of the English Church, *A Library of Fathers of the Catholic Church,* Oxford, 1857, pps. 747–748.

tian saint![18] Nothing, surely, could expose better the Gentile ideology embedded in religious as well as non-religious types of anti-semitism.

Illustrations from patristic literature could be multiplied almost indefinitely. The above are sufficient, however, to capture the flavor of patristic ideas with regard to Judaism, including the manner in which, as time moved forward, the church became increasingly ignorant of the religious life of the synagogue, and therefore increasingly hostile in its image of the Jew. Prejudice and theology, for all practical purposes, lost any meaningful distinction. With such an attitude implanted in Christian piety during the formative centuries, the ground was thoroughly prepared for the anti-Jewish explosions of the late Middle Ages, and, according to Parkes and Isaac, for the inhuman anti-semitism of the modern world. Without the church, Hitler would not have been possible. In a private conversation with the Catholic bishop, Berning, in 1933, "Hitler . . . pointed out that the Church always had regarded the Jews as parasites and had banished them into the ghetto. He was merely going to do what the Church had done for 1,500 years."[19] The fact that Bishop Berning apparently could not refute the German Chancellor's logic is, in essence, the case against Christianity.

But Christianity has not been without its defenders as well. The case for the church can be summarized as resting on three arguments: firstly, that the New Testament, to which Christian theology is always organically related, is not an anti-semitic book; secondly, that most, if not all religious enmity toward Judaism owes its origins to pagan rather than Christian sources; and, thirdly, that the religious substructure of modern racialist

18. "But prosaic Pontius Pilate must become a hero to satisfy the mediaeval hagiographer. Lacunae always invited his attention. The silence of his sources was a veritable deus ex machina. The mediaeval myth-maker had in Pilate a subject which could easily be touched up." Conrad Moehlman, *The Christian-Jewish Tragedy, A Study in Religious Prejudice*, Rochester, 1933, p. 45.

19. Lewy, *op. cit.*, p. 51.

anti-semitism is incidental when compared with the non-religious forces which victimized the Jews in modern society. Each of these points must be examined briefly.

As one element in a general Christian response to Auschwitz, the New Testament is being subjected to a new and careful scrutiny today. Jews, not surprisingly, have long been sensitive to certain passages which the patristic theologians and their heirs utilized as the scriptural basis for their disdain. Thus, in particular, Matthew 27:25,[20] I Thessalonians 2:14–16,[21] and much of the Gospel of John[22] have acquired notoriety as so-called "proofs" of the deicide-character of Judaism and the curse under which Jews perpetuate their existence throughout the ages. John, especially, has commonly been labelled the "father of anti-semitism."

How just is the accusation that the New Testament is the root of the problem, that is, the real source of the hostility which Jews, obliged to live in a Christian culture, have been forced to endure? At this point, the defenders of Christianity tend to divide into two camps. Some, like Gregory Baum, deny categorically that the Christian scriptures are in any sense anti-semitic: ". . . Jules Isaac accuses primarily the fourth gospel and certain passages of Matthew as having been written with a view to shifting the entire responsibility for Jesus' crucifixion on to the Jews and of making this crime against justice appear like the people's final rejection of God's message. . . . The supposition however is one which a Christian must reject, and reject vehemently."[23]

20. "And all the people answered, 'His blood be on us and on our children!' " (RSV).
21. "For you, brethren, became imitators of the churches of God in Christ Jesus which are in Judea; for you suffered the same things from your own countrymen as they did from the Jews, who killed both the Lord Jesus and the prophets, and drove us out, and displease God and oppose all men . . ." (RSV).
22. Especially John 5:17–47; 6:41–59; 7:14–24; 8:21–59. These constitute four tirades against the Jews.
23. Gregory Baum, The Jews and the Gospel, A Re-Examination of the New Testament, London and Glen Rock, 1961, p. 4.

According to Baum, whose own explorations are devoted to the task, any seemingly offensive section of the New Testament can be explained satisfactorily in other terms,[24] usually whereby the Jew is seen less as a Jew than as a universal human prototype.

Other Christian scholars (mostly Protestants), however, are more willing to acknowledge the presence of distinct anti-Jewish sentiments in the New Testament, but insist that these must be interpreted in their proper historical setting, as polemical reflections of the mutual animosity between the church and the synagogue toward the end of the first century. Once this fact is understood, it only remains to separate the essential gospel from its accidental human expression during an unfortunate time of troubles in order to show that Christianity is not really antisemitic. Perhaps Krister Stendahl may be considered as typical of this view. Stendahl, however, worries about the capacity of unsophisticated Christians to make the necessary distinctions. "Nor does it quite suffice to stress the love of Christ as an antidote to the bitter language about the Jews to which the Christian biblereader is exposed . . . This is the really serious level of Christian anti-Semitism: can the church admit to the tinge of anti-Jewish elements in its very Scriptures?"[25]

The latter approach (probably the sounder) obviously concedes some ground to the accusers of Christianity. Although not fundamentally an anti-semitic textbook, the New Testament nonetheless is tainted. To a later, post-apostolic generation of theologians, ill-disposed toward the Jews to begin with, sufficient anti-Jewish material was available in its pages to feed the fires of their prejudice with religious passion. Of course, other texts which breathe a different spirit toward Judaism are also to be found, for example, Romans 9–11, even if personal warmth

24. Baum has recently revised his original book, now published under the title, *Is the New Testament Anti-Semitic?* The changes, although in a liberal direction, are nonetheless minor.
25. Krister Stendahl, "Judaism and Christianity: A Plea for a New Relationship," *Cross Currents* (Vol. XVII/no. 4/Fall 1967), p. 450.

rather than theological approval dominates these chapters (more will be said about Romans 9–11 later). But, as Stendahl declares, the "bitter language" cannot be robbed of its sting just by balancing the good against the bad. Hence, this qualifying view fails to exonerate the church, because of the evil use to which the tainted passages have been put in Christian history. Only too often, as in the case of the passion dramas still performed annually at Oberammergau, Germany,[26] an uncritical rendition of much of the New Testament—especially an uncritical rendition of the Johannine literature wrenched from its historical context—has served the cause of anti-semitism. Few persons, apart from professional scholars, possess the critical acumen to keep the historic circumstances surrounding the dangerous texts firmly in mind. The average man hears such lines as Matthew 27:25 in a direct and immediate sense only.

While the church has been harsh in its treatment of Jews, the second argument maintains that the real fault does not lie in Christian piety *per se,* but rather in the pagan animosity which Christians unwittingly baptized into the church when their religion officially conquered the Roman Empire. In the judgment of Fadiey Lovsky, a French authority, many of the slanders characteristic of Christian popular anti-semitism were anticipated in the pre-Christian anti-Jewish feeling of the Hellenistic world.[27] Thus, Lovsky insists, the social climate was infected long before patristic theology formulated its theological portrait of the Jew, and even this portrait owes as much to its pagan antecedents as to its Christian sources. For example, non-Christian versions of the malediction motif have been traced, rightly or wrongly, in the writings of pagan anti-semites such as Philostratus and Apion.[28]

26. Based on John's Gospel.
27. Fadiey Lovsky, *Antisémitisme et Mystère d'Israel,* Paris, 1955, p. 66.
28. Philip C. Deever, *The Anti-Judaism of the New Testament in the Light of Its Biblical and Hellenistic Context,* unpublished Th.D. dissertation, Union Theological Seminary, New York, 1958, p. 57.

Various other Christian historians have similarly taken pains to emphasize that pagan anti-semitism was "neither an artificial nor insignificant development but rather a substantial one, grave in potentialities."[29]

On the basis of this assertion, it has been customary for Christian apologists to link ancient paganism with modern paganism; the Nazi racialist, in other words, is interpreted more or less plausibly as a reincarnation of the ancient anti-semite in twentieth-century guise—a logical step that effectively excuses the church of any real culpability. Thus, we read: "The anti-Jewish outlook found in the ecclesiastical tradition is not the starting point of modern, racial anti-semitism; this has been said over and over again by Christian apologists, and rightly so. . . . It was only when the type of 'the Jews' created by Christian preaching is filled with pagan hatred, coming from sources which have nothing to do with Christianity, that we have the passion of modern anti-semitism."[30]

Is this argument valid? Interestingly enough, it finds support in unusual places. Freud, as we have seen, without knowing much about either theology or history, believed that anti-semitism represents in part the vengeance of the suppressed "pagan" inside every Gentile Christian against the Jewish deity in whose name he (that is, his ancestors) were forcibly baptized.[31] Because

29. Edward H. Flannery, *The Anguish of the Jews, Twenty-Three Centuries of Anti-Semitism,* New York, 1965.

Flannery's study of anti-semitism, the first by a Catholic historian, produced some reaction in both Jewish and Christian circles. Although highly praised for his intentions and his objectivity, Flannery was also criticized for injecting a measure of Catholic apologetics into his history.

See the symposium on the subject by Eliezer Berkovits, Arthur Hertzberg, Erich Isaac, Gavin I. Langmuir, Jacob Neusner, Howard Nemerov, Leon Poliakov, Steven S. Schwarzschild, in the journal *Continuum* (Vol. IV/No. 3/Autumn 1966), pps. 417–442.

30. Baum, *op. cit.,* p. 3.

31. Freud, *op. cit.,* p. 117. For a similar view, see Maurice Samuel, *The Great Hatred,* New York, 1940, pps. 127–128. Like Freud, Samuel is a Jewish thinker.

the majority of ex-pagan Christians really detest the church on an unconscious level, the Jew becomes a convenient symbol for working out these lurking feelings of hatred. Freud, of course, was Jewish himself, and a refugee from Hitler as well; he certainly had no stake in Christian apologetics, but his theory must remain a theory—it cannot be accepted as proof of an argument that is historical in nature, and must stand or fall according to the evidence of history.

More recently, however, a Jewish historian, Arthur Hertzberg, has provided this argument with some novel historical support. In an important study of French Jewry during the era of the Enlightenment, Hertzberg seeks to demonstrate that the anti-Judaism of pagan antiquity was revived by the *philosophes* of the eighteenth century, especially by Voltaire (who imagined himself as a Cicero *redivivus*), and directly transmitted to later racialist theorists. "The vital link, the man who skipped over the Christian centuries and provided a new, international, secular anti-Jewish rhetoric in the name of European culture rather than religion, was Voltaire."[32] Hertzberg's thesis has stirred a measure of controversy, and may represent an overstatement. If, however, he should be right about Voltaire, one must conclude that the pagan heritage played a larger role in the evolution of modern anti-semitism than is usually believed. But it does not follow that the whole matter can be explained in these terms.

A reading of the typical charges raised against the Jews by pagan anti-semites certainly confirms the view that pre-Christian animosity was not a minor affair. Josephus, the Jewish historian of antiquity, was sufficiently alarmed by the appeal which contemporary anti-Jewish writers enjoyed as to compose his own refutations. He found it necessary to defend the Jews against such accusations as having been fathered by lepers, having illegally established themselves in Alexandria, having acted seditiously, having worshipped the head of an ass (in the holy of holies),

32. Hertzberg, *The French Enlightenment and the Jews,* p. 313.

having engaged in the sacrificial murder of Greeks, having sworn themselves to detest all foreigners, especially Greeks, having delighted in impiety and evil laws, having no wise men, and so on.[33] Even Parkes is forced to admit that the entry into the church of the already anti-Jewish Roman upper classes in the fourth century provided "the soil on which the hostility of the church fathers found it easy to sow seed."[34] In all probability, some of the roots of western anti-semitism are pagan in origin, coming, as Lovsky declares, from "an arsenal of calumnies," which did not even require translation from Greek to Latin in order to permeate the Roman world.[35]

But at least two dangers present themselves if this argument is adopted in too unqualified a fashion. The first danger is that of underestimating the purely religious hostility between Christians and Jews as the church and the synagogue drew more and more apart in the twilight of the apostolic age. If pagan anti-semitism was baptized into the church, it must have fused with anti-Jewish feelings already present, and in the process of hardening. Whether, on the other hand, the religious rivalry between the two communities would have eroded eventually, had a wedding not been consummated between pagan and Christian prejudice, is impossible to determine. Christians probably should not give themselves the benefit of the doubt.

The second danger is on a different level: that of definition. The word "pagan" tends to carry a negative connotation in the Christian religious vocabulary, and, for this reason, offers a subtle temptation. It is relatively easy for the church to disassociate "true" Christianity from persecutions inflicted on the Jews for the semantic reason that Christians, by definition, are incapable of committing pagan cruelties. In this way, the issue of Christian

33. Flavius Josephus, *Contra Apion*, Book II, 1–15, trans. in *Complete Works of Josephus*, Vol. X, World Syndicate Publishing Co., pps. 470–497.
34. Parkes, *CCS*, p. 138.
35. Lovsky, *loc. cit.*

guilt is side-stepped adroitly. This, surely, is the fallacy in Baum's assertion that the type of the Jew created by Christian preaching requires the infusion of "pagan" hatred before it can become anti-semitism. Would it not be more honest for Christians to acknowledge that religious fanaticism, as a corruption of a zeal for the gospel, does not need extraneous influences in order to turn to prejudice and persecution?

The second argument in defense of Christianity, therefore, while stronger than the first, does not allow the church to escape without censure. Christendom, in the final analysis, is still responsible for having permitted the latent anti-Judaism of the pre-Christian world to stain its life and faith.

The third argument either denies or minimizes the religious sources of anti-semitism in favor of a non-religious historical explanation, usually in terms of economic factors. Although not a Christian herself, and certainly without interest in assuming the mantle of a Christian apologist, Hannah Arendt is probably its most impressive advocate. "The charge against Christianity in general, with its two thousand years of history, cannot be proved, and if it could be proved, it would be horrible."[36] Arendt, as we have mentioned, traces the evolution of modern anti-semitism through an analysis of European history especially in the nineteenth century in which a tragic destiny is plotted by secular forces for the Jew. Her evidence is impressive, but not conclusive. Most likely, the issue between Arendt and, for example, Isaac, whose evidence is also impressive, has no simple resolution. It is not possible to pursue this debate exhaustively; rather, we must content ourselves with the observation that both writers appear to have grasped important aspects of the truth. Psychologically, however, Christians with troubled consciences would beyond any question be more comfortable in believing that Arendt has come closer to the heart of the problem. But Hertzberg's criticism of Arendt is persuasive: ". . . is it conceivable that the enormous power of

36. Hannah Arendt, *Eichmann in Jerusalem*, p. 297.

this hatred was bred in a few short decades?"[37] The violence of recent anti-semitism has been too great to be explained as the simple product of social and political stresses in modern times. A deeper dimension is also involved. Although understandably tempted, the church would be unwise to take refuge behind the type of argument constructed in *The Origins of Totalitarianism* as a means of avoiding an otherwise unavoidable indictment. The moral as well as the intellectual snares of this course are immense. It is better to face the indictment.

The case against Christianity has to be modified, but it still remains. No verdict of "not guilty" is possible, even if the exact degree of Christian guilt is indeterminate. Berkovits is not altogether right, but neither is he entirely in the wrong. Undoubtedly, he is closer to the truth than the complacent defenders of a church regarded as spotless and without sin.

37. Hertzberg, *op. cit.*, p. 7.

IV. Catholic Theology in Evolution

(1) The Traditionalists

Christian theology has been intimately connected with anti-semitism since the patristic era. A critical introspection, therefore, is the paramount duty of the post-Auschwitz Christian mind. This, and the succeeding chapters, will take soundings in contemporary theology, beginning with Roman Catholicism.

It must be deemed among the most impressive facts of the present time that much of the initiative in the revitalization of the Christian church is now coming from Catholic sources. This is true of theology in all its aspects, and especially true of the encounter of Jews and Christians, where, in the late sixties, Protestants (one forms the impression) have lagged seriously behind. As no less a voice than Karl Barth has prophesied, it is not inconceivable that Protestantism, which derives its being from the principle of reform, might be forced to surrender pride of place to the supposedly ossified spirit of Catholic Christianity.[1] Certainly, many Catholic theologians have demonstrated a new and at times creative interest in the problems of a Jewish-Chris-

1. Karl Barth, "Roman Catholicism: A Question to the Protestant Church," *Theology and Church, Shorter Writings 1920–1928*, translated by Louise Pettibone Smith, London and New York, 1962, p. 314.

68

tian dialogue, and have struggled to redefine the church's understanding of Judaism. Slowly and painfully, an awareness that traditional ideas are ineradicably tainted with anti-semitism has arisen. The purpose of this (and the next) chapter is to trace the metamorphosis in Catholic thinking in the mid-twentieth century under the impact of the Nazi explosion against the Jews.

Catholic doctrinal teaching concerning Judaism has its foundations in the opinions of the early fathers and their medieval heirs. The essence of the patristic viewpoint lies in the post-apostolic substitution of the "new" (or sometimes "true") Israel, the church, for the "old" (or "false") Israel, that is, Judaism after the resurrection.[2] In this manner, the Jews were unceremoniously dismissed from the ongoing stream of saving events called by modern theology "salvation history." We have already seen, through examples from patristic literature, that this theme developed in an increasingly anti-semitic vein as the church moved away from its original Jewish matrix. Part, also, of the patristic doctrine was rooted in eschatology: the belief, based on Romans 9–11, that the Jews, despite their fall from grace, would be preserved by God in order that their conversion could signal the end of temporal history. This belief, incidentally, came to the rescue of the synagogue more than once during the Middle Ages, since it prevented the hand of persecution from turning to actual annihilation when religious fanaticism reached its zenith. Other aspects of Paul's thought, however, notably his compassion for his "kinsmen by race," sunk into abeyance.

Ideas formulated in the early Christian centuries remained for the most part firmly fixed in the Catholic mind until the eve of Auschwitz. Medieval and modern theologians merely embroidered the patristic doctrine. In the thirteenth century, for example, Pope Innocent III, inspired by the malediction motif, wrote as follows: "The Lord made Cain a wanderer and a fugi-

2. The term "new Israel" is not biblical, but apparently owes its origin to second-century Christian ecclesiastical doctrine. Documented in Marcel Simon, *Verus Israel, Étude sur les Relations entre Chrétiens et Juifs dans l'Empire Romain,* Paris, 1948.

tive over the earth, but set a mark upon him, making his head to shake, lest any finding him should slay him. Thus the Jews, against whom the blood of Jesus Christ calls out, although they ought not to be killed, lest the Christian people forget the Divine Law, yet as wanderers ought they to remain upon the earth, until their countenance be filled with shame and they seek the name of Jesus Christ the Lord."[3]

In the seventeenth century, Jacques Bossuet, Bishop of Meaux in France, echoed in almost identical terms the same patristic motif. "By this profound design of God, the Jews subsist still in the midst of the nations, where they are dispersed and captive: but they subsist according to the character of their reprobation, visibly fallen through their infidelity from the promises made to the fathers, banished from the promised land, no longer having any land to cultivate, slaves wherever they are, without honour, without liberty, without any form as a people."[4]

In the twentieth century, Cardinal Faulhaber, preaching in a Germany already half-hypnotized by Hitler, nonetheless saw no evil in the patristic legacy: "After the death of Christ Israel was dismissed from the service of Revelation. She had not known the time of her visitation. She had repudiated and rejected the Lord's Anointed, had driven Him to the Cross. Then the veil of the Temple was rent, and with it the covenant between the Lord and His people. The Daughters of Sion received the bill of divorce, and from that time forth Assuerus wanders, for ever restless, over the face of the earth."[5]

3. Cited (with Latin text) by Solomon Grayzel, *The Church and the Jews in the XIIIth Century, A study of their relations during the years 1198–1254*. Based on the Papal Letters and Conciliar Decrees of the Period. Dropsie College for Hebrew and Cognate Learning, Philadelphia, 1933, p. 127.
4. Jacques Bossuet, *Discours sur l'histoire universelle*, imprimé pour Samuel Bagster, Londres, 1807, pps. 286–287. My translation.
5. Michael von Faulhaber, *Judaism, Christianity and Germany*, trans. by George D. Smith, New York, 1934, p. 5.
It seems to me that Lewy is justified when he comments: "It, there-

CATHOLIC THEOLOGY IN EVOLUTION

That was in 1933! Faulhaber, though, was not personally an anti-semite. He simply made no connection between anti-semitism and Catholic theology, and, in this respect, typified the church perfectly. On an official level, at least, the latter registered awareness of anti-semitism as a moral danger through a decree issued by the Holy Office in 1928. Anti-semitism was condemned as unworthy of Christians "just as every kind of envy and jealousy among the nations must be disapproved."[6] Again, in the encyclical *Mit brennender Sorge* (1937), the papacy made the same point with greater passion. "Whoever exalts race, or the people, or the State, or a particular form of State, or the depositories of power, or any other fundamental value of the human community . . . whoever raises these notions above their standard value and divinizes them to an idolatrous level, distorts and perverts an order of the world planned and created by God: he is far from the true faith in God and from the concept of life which that faith upholds."[7]

Still, however, no suggestion of Christian complicity in anti-semitism, and especially no criticism of any Christian doctrine, even occurred, one gathers, to the ecclesiastical authorities. Not even the famous utterance of Pius XI to a visiting group of Belgian pilgrims in 1938—"Spiritually we are Semites"[8]—reveals any papal insight into the real dimensions of the problem. Christianity and anti-semitism were regarded as two independent and wholly unrelated entities.

Yet, glimmerings of a connection were not far from the horizon. It was not possible to reaffirm the Jewish character of the Christian faith, as the pope did in 1938, without potentially

---

fore, is little short of a falsification of history when Faulhaber's sermons in 1933 are hailed by one recent Catholic writer as a 'condemnation of the persecution of the Jews.' "

Lewy, *op. cit.,* p. 276.

6. *Acta Apostolica Sedia,* XX (1928), 104.

7. *The Papal Encyclicals in Their Historical Context,* edited by Anne Fremantle, New York, 1956, p. 251.

8. First reported in *La Croix,* no. 17060, September 17, 1938.

71

bringing under judgment the anti-Jewish elements embedded in Catholic tradition. Sooner or later, someone was bound to realize this fact. Hence, in 1942, Henri De Lubac came closer to a moment of truth. "The faith of Abraham is already our faith. In its fundamental precepts, the law of Moses is still our law. The great men of Israel are truly our fathers. The prophets still rouse us today to the great lessons that God has charged them to deliver to his people. They console us in our distress and awaken hope in us. The mildness of the breeze in which the Spirit visited Elijah announces to us the mildness of our Christ. The 'denunciations' of Amos stimulate us to justice, whereas Hosea prepares our hearts for love. The majesty of the God of Isaiah makes us fall prostrate with him before the thrice-holy Face. Jeremiah creates a new dimension in our hearts. Job exhorts us to a virile patience. The Psalms nourish our prayers each day. Daniel and the Maccabees teach us fidelity."[9]

The *Sitz im Leben* of this unusual rhapsody was a protest against the "new religious front" of Vichy France in the 1940's, which sought to aryanize Christianity after the Germanic model. De Lubac, sensing the peril threatening the church, was moved to celebrate the Jewish character of Christian piety in conscious polemical terms. The result was nothing less than spiritual self-discovery, together with the establishment, in embryo form, of a critical principle within Catholic theology for testing the purity of the church's own faith. If Christians are truly this close in spirit to Judaism, there can be no room for anti-Jewish dogmas of any description in Catholic teaching.

The logic of this conclusion, however, has been slow in penetrating the Catholic mind. Even with a reborn conscience in the face of modern anti-semitism, Catholic thinkers have experienced difficulty in weaning themselves from the patristic tradition. Can the old wineskins of patristic theology be patched sufficiently in order to contain the new wine of a rediscovered Christian semi-

9. De Lubac, *op. cit.,* p. 38. My translation.

tism? Or must they burst altogether under its ferment? To answer this question, we are obliged to examine some representative post-Auschwitz theologians. Those described in this chapter are the traditionalists. That is to say, they represent an attempt to preserve the old in a new context, reconciling patristic ideas with the moral and intellectual crisis that anti-semitism has posed for the Christian church. Although their writings display considerable theological ingenuity, they testify to the innate resistance of Christian faith to radical change.

The first theologian on our list is a woman: a French convert from Judaism to Catholicism, who, in spite of her background, has produced the most conservative statement on the subject in post-war Catholic theology of which I am aware. Yet D. Judant's book, *Les Deux Israel,* was composed in the shadow of the holocaust, and is fully cognizant of Jewish suffering. In light of this suffering, her desire is to explain and defend a true Catholic interpretation of the Jewish role in history, as the latter is revealed in scripture and tradition. Like all traditionalists, her approach to the problem is strictly on a dogmatic basis: "The explosion of unjustifiable hate of the Nazis ought not to cause a blind sentimentality which, based on an inordinate charity, fails to take account of indisputable scriptural or theological ideas."[10] Charity (or love) is not to be ignored, but truth comes first. "There can be no contradiction between truth and charity: there is no charity which does not rest on truth."[11] In other words, according to this theologian, the Christian need not worry too much about ethics as long as he gets his theology rightly defined. To know the truth, presumably, is to do it.

The last statement has a measure of plausibility, until one learns that, in Judant's view, the "truth" in question is the same theological tradition which was given definitive shape by the

10. D. Judant, *Les deux Israel, Essai sur le mystère du salut selon l'économie des deux Testaments,* Paris, 1960, p. 16. My translation.
11. *Ibid.,* p. 17. My translation.

early fathers and incorporated into the time-honored teaching of Catholic Christianity. Not everything, she acknowledges, that the fathers said is to be accorded equal authority; after all, at times they did sound a little extreme, having to protect the faith of Christians against "dangerous influences."[12] Nonetheless, for the modern Catholic no less than for the ancient Catholic, the patristic position remains authoritative, and no real deviation is permissible. Judant's theological opinion of Judaism, as a consequence, is thoroughly traditionalist in every respect. Her theology reveals a somewhat desperate squeezing of the new wine of a post-Auschwitz Christian conscience into old and hopelessly inadequate wineskins, to the detriment of the former.

Thus, she begins where the patristic age began, accepting as axiomatic the assumption that Judaism, after the resurrection, was stripped of all religious meaning. "It is not possible to think that after the coming of Christ Israel according to the flesh remained in any sense the people of God. The theology of the church is based on exactly this replacement of the old Israel by the new."[13] Different patristic writers developed this doctrine differently, depending on the degree of anti-Jewish animus which they felt, but, allowing for the variations, the essential position must be considered as fixed for all time. The Jews, as Aquinas declared, are *"exiderant a gratia"*;[14] that is the sum of the matter.

But Judant, one must hasten to add, is not an anti-semite. She refrains, for example, from approving the cruel accusations of deicide and malediction, although these are interwoven with patristic theology. ". . . Catholic doctrine has always shown that both Jews and Gentiles—that is to say, the two great biblical categories of humanity—share responsibility for the Passion."[15] Nor have the Jews been cursed by God: "This rigorous inter-

12. *Ibid.,* p. 133.
13. *Ibid.,* p. 123. My translation.
14. *Ibid.,* p. 135.
15. *Ibid.,* p. 51. My translation.

pretation is not exact, although a good number of the fathers of the church employ the expression of a 'cursed people.' No phrase of the New Testament implies this sense, not even the most severe condemnations."[16]

Yet, in spite of this disclaimer, Judant still believes that the Jews are the bearers of a special guilt, to which their history after 70 A.D. in some manner testifies. "The sin of Israel was shared, but it exists; it was not cancelled because the Gentiles participated as well."[17] The source of this guilt lay in the Jewish refusal to recognize in Jesus the messiah whom they awaited. "If they had not been deceived by their longing for a temporal messianic age, if they had aspired to the spiritual liberation which their prophets had foretold, their position would have been different."[18] While the responsibility for not accepting Jesus did not rest in equal measure upon each individual Jew, nonetheless, as Judant sees things, the whole Jewish community was collectively involved. "Can one think that only the authorities were guilty when the mass was without responsibility?—No, because the people as a whole ratified the attitude of the high priests and the elders."[19] This collective involvement, moreover, has been perpetuated in the attitude of disbelief ("*perfidia*") which has been typical of most Jews since their initial act of spiritual treason. Hence, even if the deicide charge is dropped, the stigma of religious guilt is retained. "In begging Jerusalem to turn to its God: *Jerusalem, Jerusalem, convertere ad Dominum Deum tuum,* the church implores at the same time the conversion of both Jews and Christians (unfaithful also), but the infidelity of the first is more strongly emphasized; that of the second is relative."[20]

Not only does the unique guilt of the Jews continue, but the

16. *Ibid.,* pps. 111–112. My translation.
17. *Ibid.,* p. 54. My translation.
18. *Ibid.,* p. 115. My translation.
19. *Ibid.,* pps. 46–47. My translation.
20. *Ibid.,* p. 55. My translation.

vicissitudes of Jewish history are interpreted in light of their spiritual obtuseness. Judant is too dominated by patristic ideas not to think in this fashion. Two events in particular appear to her as "disturbing facts": the suppression of Jewish independence only forty years after the crucifixion, and the mysterious preservation of the Jewish people in their homeless situation since that time. "We have here, beyond any doubt, a particular aspect of the 'mystery' and destiny of Israel."[21] To explain this mystery, she invokes, like a good scholastic, Augustine's famous description of the Jews as unwilling witnesses to the truth of Christianity (contained in the latter's *Enarrationes in Psalmos*).[22] "As one sees, in the thought of Augustine, the punishment of the Jews, their dispersion, is related to their condition as the witness-people in the face of the church."[23]

Augustine's doctrine, however, amounts to little more than a theological elaboration of the malediction idea, giving this rather crude accusation a measure of intellectual respectability. For this reason, any modern attempt to explicate the fate of the Jews in an Augustinian frame of reference has obvious dangers. Here, as elsewhere, Judant's commitment to the patristic corpus as the final word of Catholic truth betrays her. Following the example of the church fathers, she argues from history, but rejects ordinary historical explanations for her "disturbing facts" on the empirical level. With less excuse than the earliest Christian thinkers, she twists history in order to prove a theological point.

But, as we have said, Judant is not an anti-semite. That is the pathos of her book. She condemns, like all post-Auschwitz theologians, "an anti-Jewish prejudice incompatible with the Christian spirit (and especially with the thought of St. Paul, who was

21. *Ibid.*, p. 144. My translation.
22. St. Augustine, *Enarrationes in Psalmos*, translated in *The Nicene and Post-Nicene Fathers*, edited by Philip Schaff, The Christian Literature Co., New York, 1888, Vol. VIII, p. 227.
23. Judant, *op. cit.*, p. 145. My translation.

proud of his Jewish origin)."[24] Even Aquinas himself, the great Catholic doctor, does not escape her censure when in places he seemed to forget that the church is composed of Jews as well as Gentiles.[25] Judant's willingness to correct Aquinas in light of Paul (Romans 9–11) reflects the general tendency of her study to favor, whenever possible, the side of patristic theology which shows the least antipathy toward the Jews. In spite of their spiritual destitution, she feels, the ex-people of God are more readily grafted to their "true olive-tree" (that is, the church) than Gentile converts.[26] Whatever degree of Pauline philo-semitism which the fathers did not see fit to suppress breaks through fairly strongly, especially with regard to God's eventual mercy at the end of history. Nevertheless, when Judant's contribution to the post-Auschwitz theological renaissance in Catholic attitudes toward Judaism is assessed, little that is good can be said. Not the new wine of revolution, but the old wineskins of reaction win an easy victory.

A theologian of far greater consequence, although his major study of the problem is fifteen years older than Judant's, is (Cardinal) Charles Journet. As an erudite attempt to justify the patristic tradition in the midst of what he describes as "the most terrible assault of violence, scorn and savage cruelty planned against Israel that the world has ever seen,"[27] *Destinées d'Israel* is a powerful book. It is, however, deeply conservative in its presuppositions. Like Judant, Journet's mind is torn between two forces: a revulsion against anti-semitism and a commitment to Catholic "truth." Like Judant also he begins with the premise that theological dogma, because the Catholic alone understands the secret of the Jewish identity, provides the only true hope of defeating anti-semitism. Once again, therefore, charity becomes essen-

24. *Ibid.*, p. 181. My translation.
25. *Ibid.*, p. 190.
26. *Ibid.*, p. 192.
27. Charles Journet, *Destinées d'Israel, A propos du Salut par les Juifs*, Paris, 1945, p. 9. My translation.

tially an addendum to truth, and, at least in terms of methodology, a secondary consideration. If scripture is rightly interpreted in light of tradition, charitable impulses will naturally accompany the Christian expositor as he unfolds the mysteries of revelation to his Jewish contemporaries. For Journet, moreover, the conclusions of the patristic age constitute the indispensable clue to sound doctrine, as they do for Judant.[28] Yet, throughout *Destinées d'Israel,* one can detect the presence of a larger sympathy as well as a more sensitive and informed treatment of the patristic writings than evinces itself in the rigid scholasticisms of Judant. Journet is obviously a much better scholar. Nevertheless, the traditionalist accent is the same.

Not surprisingly, Journet's theological portrait of Judaism rests on the already familiar patristic distinction between the old and new Israel, otherwise expressed in the contrast between the "Israel of the spirit" (the church) and the "Israel of the flesh" (the synagogue).[29] The Jews, accordingly, are conceived as existing under the shadow of a decisive "no" to God's self-revelation in Jesus Christ which they uttered "at the most solemn hour of their history and all the history of the world."[30] The results of this fatal decision are incalculable, for the "Israel of the exile,"[31] to which their negative response gave birth, was an Israel whose spiritual and historical destiny had been radically changed from God's original intention. "Nevertheless the spiritual consequences of this dreadful scorn were bound to spread themselves throughout the centuries. Israel was cast into a religious condition which began as deviant, and which made it hard for her to see any longer in their true aspect the pure, mysterious and authentic

28. Lovsky writes: "La position de Mgr. Journet . . . est d'une théologie prudente et volontiers conservatrice, plus patristique que biblique."

F. Lovsky, "Les Chrétiens devant Israel," 10e Cahier d'Études Juives (No. 4/1961), p. 99.

29. Journet, *op. cit.,* p. 21.

30. *Ibid.,* p. 133. My translation.

31. *Ibid.*

meaning of the promises of which she was the bearer . . ."[32] In this style, Journet portrays the pathos of the ex-people of God as a "fallen church"[33] ("*église précipitée*"), from which the immediate approval if not the eschatological mercy of God has been withdrawn. To be a Jew becomes a profound spiritual tragedy.

While Journet lends no conscious support to a deliberate anti-semitism—there is no reason for doubting the sincerity of his horror in the face of Auschwitz—,[34] the same allegiance to patristic ideas that compromises Judant's theology also has a destructive effect on Journet's otherwise sympathetic mind. Israel's "no" to Christ inevitably transforms itself into a guilty act embracing the totality of the Jewish nation. "The fault of Israel is a collective fault, committed first of all by the authorities and leaders of Israel . . . in which the majority of the crowd gathered in Jerusalem for the feast of Passover, without realizing exactly what they were doing, nevertheless shared in an alarming manner . . ."[35] To Journet, moreover, the guilt is not confined to the actors in the passion drama. The disbelief which induced first-century Judaism to repudiate its messiah remains a lasting trait of all Jews, past and present, who have failed to find their spiritual home in the church.

"In characterizing the prevarication of Israel as infidelity (*perfidia*) . . . the fathers and scholastics sought to understand it not under its most passionate, momentary and impious aspect, but, contrariwise, under its most universal, definable, socially transmissible and durable aspect."[36] A distinction is drawn, to be sure, between the modern Jew who has merely inherited a "patrimony of infidelity,"[37] and the historical community which

32. *Ibid.*, p. 136. My translation.
33. *Ibid.*, p. 148.
34. *Ibid.*, pps. 190–201.
35. *Ibid.*, pps. 134–135. My translation.
36. *Ibid.*, pps. 143–144. My translation.
37. *Ibid.*, p. 146.

actually rejected Jesus, but this does not alter the fact that the entire Jewish people in time and space is categorized under this heading. In spite of Journet's reluctance to endorse the deicide accusation, therefore, it is doubtful if this theologian really modifies the depth of Jewish guilt to any meaningful extent.

In common with Judant, Journet, in true patristic fashion, cannot refrain from tracing a hidden connection between the *perfidia* of the Jews and their historical misfortunes, although he dismisses as sub-Christian the notion that Jewish history stands under a divine curse. "The old economy of grace united too closely the spiritual and the carnal for the infidelity of Israel not to end in temporal catastrophe."[38] Hence, like the fathers, he assigns the disaster of 70 A.D., and its aftermath, to the spiritual ruin entailed in the repudiation of Christ. "The ruin of Jerusalem . . . represents nothing but the negative side of God's judgment."[39] Once again, we find reiterated the Augustinian doctrine that the Jews, rootless and homeless, are unwilling witnesses through their lot to the truth of Christianity. "The ambiguity of Israel's destiny was recognized by the fathers . . . Their apologetic concern to appeal to the prophets . . . led them to think that the main purpose of the hardening of the Jews was to bear throughout the world the scriptures which witnessed to the messiah whom they had crucified and to the faith which they detested."[40]

In spite of the centuries between the patristic age and the present time, Journet has no trouble in following the patristic argument *simpliciter;* his theology, as a consequence, reduces itself to another example of the type of providential reading of history which misinterprets concrete events in order to prove its own assumptions. If there is any improvement in this mode of

38. *Ibid.,* p. 167. My translation.
39. *Ibid.,* p. 168. My translation. Like Bossuet, Journet believes that the early destruction of Jerusalem under Nebuchadnezzar was a typological prophecy of the future fate of the Jews.
40. *Ibid.,* p. 160. My translation.

thinking over an unadulterated charge of malediction, it is clearly very slight. The lesson that emerges is the same lesson that we drew from Judant's study: contemporary Catholic theologians who, for intellectual or emotional reasons, feel themselves tied to the umbilical cord of traditional theology cannot write an enlightened Christian doctrine of Judaism morally acceptable to the twentieth century, no matter how great their revulsion against anti-semitism. The impulse to defend the thought-patterns of the past is, in this context, self-defeating if one also aspires after reform.

It is the irony of Journet's long essay that its author is passionately opposed to anti-semitism. His main purpose is to demonstrate the place still reserved for the Jews in the divine economy of grace. He speaks of the "epiphany of the catholicity of the church,"[41] meaning by this awkward phrase the supreme event toward which all time is moving: the final fusion of Jews and Gentiles together in one people of God. Nor does Journet neglect Paul. Paul's love for his fellow Jews is also Journet's love, and redeems in some measure the patristic stamp of his theology. In purely human terms, the Jews are less to be blamed than pitied in their spiritual decrepitude. Indeed, by the "too frequent hypocrisy of their Christian life,"[42] the Christian peoples are more often at fault than the fallen house of Israel for the Jewish failure to accept Christianity. As restless searchers after truth, moreover, the Jews still fulfill a valuable world-historical role (before the consummation) that Christians seldom recognize.

With these and similar ideas, his book concludes. In intention at least, some new wine is present. But the old wineskins have survived intact.

A Catholic too famous to be ignored, from whom even Journet has derived some of his views, is the self-styled "old

41. *Ibid.*, pps. 356f.
42. *Ibid.*, p. 184.

layman" of French Catholicism, Jacques Maritain. A literary protégé of the older French writer, Léon Bloy,[43] Maritain showed his theological preoccupation with the Jews early in his career. Toward anti-semitism in every shade from the Dreyfus affair until Nazism, he has long been an implacable foe. "I say that in a time wherein anti-Semitic persecutions have assumed an unheard of proportion, wherein thousands upon thousands of miserable people have been put outside the law, subjected to brutalities and humiliations beyond description, to slow death, to the 'spontaneous' violence of the mob or to the horrors of concentration camps . . . in such a time the only *realism* which matters . . . is not to speak a word, not to write a word which could serve as any excuse whatever for degrading hatred, and thereby to find oneself some day accused of the blood or despair of creatures of God."[44]

This is a great expression of Christian moral duty, but, like Judant and Journet, Maritain approaches the problem essentially as a Catholic dogmatist. For him, revealed "truth" is the proper methodological starting point. The patristic accent, moreover, is obvious in the following lines. "One day Israel stumbled and was caught in a trap; it stumbled against God,—and in what an encounter, never to be repeated! Israel did not know what it was doing; but its leaders knew that they were making their choice against God. In one of those acts of free will which involve the destiny of a whole community, the priests of Israel, the bad

43. Bloy's book, *Le Salut par les Juifs,* published in 1892, represented an attempt to oppose the rampant anti-semitism of contemporary France, as exemplified especially by Drumont, by emphasizing the religious significance of the Jews in the Christian dispensation. "Leon Bloy sees in Israel a 'Corpus Mysticum' . . . and finally affirms in glowing language, that the Race which begot the Redeemer will in God's good time be reconciled to Him. In this reintegration of the Jewish race, Bloy recognizes a third Age of Christianity."
Emmanuela Polimeni, *Léon Bloy the pauper prophet,* New York, 1951, p. 103. The influence on Maritain is obvious.
44. Jacques Maritain, "Answer to One Unnamed," *Ransoming the Time,* trans. by Harry Lorin Binsse, New York, 1941, p. 195.

watchers of the vineyard, the slayers of prophets, with excellent reasons of political prudence, chose the world, and to that choice their whole people was henceforth bound—until it changes of its own accord."[45] This passage could have been written by any of the fathers.

Maritain, as one would expect of a sophisticated theologian, has no use for the naked accusations of deicide and malediction; nevertheless, in a refined, quasi-philosophical fashion, he succeeds (like Journet) in blaming the Jews for their own historical troubles. "Penalty is not the arbitrary contrivance of some wound inflicted from without upon an unimpaired being to satisfy the law. It is—in the moral order itself—the fruit of the wound inflicted on a being through his own freedom voluntarily at fault, and this natural fruit *is* the satisfaction of the law. The penalty is the working out of the fault; our punishment is our choice."[46]

The application of this principle is soon made clear. It lies in the way in which the Jews have made themselves the great nuisances of western history, thereby incurring nothing but enmity from their neighbors. Maritain, in fact, is fascinated by the idea of Israel's choice of the world, rather than God, and goes to elaborate lengths in order to describe the vocational consequences of this choice. In contrast to the vocational role of the church, that is, the "supernatural and supra-temporal saving of the world,"[47] the vocational role of Judaism lies in the "*earthly leavening* of the world."[48] This means that, in spite of themselves, the Jews must still serve the divine will, striving, in a semi-conscious way, to realize the "absolute" in historical time. At its best, the Jewish groping after God is transmuted into a passion for social justice: "Here by the waters of Babylon is the sighing for the Jerusalem of Justice, here is the cry of the prophets, the expectation and the endless desire for the terrible glory

45. Maritain, "The Mystery of Israel," *op. cit.,* p. 152.
46. *Ibid.,* pps. 153–154.
47. *Ibid.,* p. 156.
48. *Ibid.*

of God."[49] At its worst, however, the same groping turns into a debased preoccupation with material goods, notably financial gain. "The will to attain the absolute in the world can assume all forms. It can . . . create that overgrowth of activity in the handling of the goods of the earth and in money making, which finds in capitalist civilization an appropriate ambience; or it can create that revolutionary impatience and that ceaseless agitation which Bernard Lazare and many other Jews liked to point out."[50] In either case, the Jews are a driven people: ". . . like some foreign substance, like a living yeast mixed into the main body, [Israel] gives the world no quiet . . . it teaches the world to be dissatisfied and restless so long as it has not God, it stimulates the movement of history."[51]

Even under the limitations of their guilty existence, says Maritain, the Jews have in some sense a positive vocation which forever sets them apart from other peoples. (At this point, according to one observer, he comes "very near to the Barthian view but fails to draw Barth's conclusions."[52]) Thus, the old wineskins show signs of being at least partially dissolved, for Maritain's imagination carries him well beyond the church fathers, who could see in Judaism no worth whatsoever, except as a foil for Christian polemics. But the substance of his doctrine remains one with Augustine, Cyprian, Eusebius and the other intellectual progenitors of the long tradition of theological anti-Judaism. At heart, Maritain is a conservative, even if his view contains some transitional elements. Unfortunately, judging from his latest writing, *The Peasant of the Garonne*,[53] the traditional-

49. *Ibid.*, pps. 160–161.
50. *Ibid.*, p. 159.
51. *Ibid.*, p. 156.
52. Jakob Jocz, *A Theology of Election, Israel and the Church*, London, 1949, p. 211, fn. 13.
53. Jacques Maritain, *The Peasant of the Garonne, An Old Layman Questions Himself about the Present Time*, trans. by Michael Cuddihy and Elizabeth Hughes, New York, 1968, p. 185.
"The Church is without stain or wrinkle . . . And I have often

84

ist side of Maritain, in this as in other things, has had the last, rather ill-tempered word.

Perhaps less conservative than Maritain, but still in the traditionalist camp, is the great scholar of Christian origins, Jean Daniélou. Daniélou, who has engaged in dialogues with such Jews as Edmund Fleg and André Chouraqui, is fully conscious of the indictment under which the church and its teaching have fallen. He has read Isaac, for example, but feels that the latter goes too far in defending Jewish innocence in connection with the crucifixion. While the Jews are not to be accused in any deicide sense, nonetheless, inspired by a "mysterious collective economy,"[54] they reject Christ. Because of this rejection, their destiny has been marked by a "mysterious sign."[55] Implied in this sign, moreover, is a definite measure of spiritual guilt, for, if Judaism had really been faithful to its divine calling, the rabbis would surely have recognized in Jesus the messiah predicted by the prophets.[56] The crux of Israel's sin, in Daniélou's view, lies in the failure of the Jewish people to accept the witness of the apostolic church to the risen Lord: "The sin of Israel was not the crucifixion of Jesus; it lies in not having believed in the resurrected Christ."[57] What happened after, not before, the resurrection is definitive.

Daniélou refuses to interpret the dispersion in the usual manner, as a punishment for the crucifixion; yet, in true orthodox fashion, he maintains that "it is not possible for us [that is, Christians] to see in contemporary Israel the people of God in the way that Israel was the people of God before Christ."[58] This

---

felt with regret . . . that Christ pardons more willingly the spits on his face than the least doubt on the holiness of his Beloved."

Nothing could be more reactionary than this extraordinary statement!

54. Jean Daniélou, *Dialogue avec Israel,* Paris, 1963, pps. 106–107.
55. *Ibid.*
56. *Ibid.,* p. 130.
57. *Ibid.,* pps. 152–153. My translation.
58. *The Jews: Views and Counterviews, A Dialogue between Jean Daniélou and André Chouraqui,* Westminster (Md.), 1967, p. 69.

credo is the great divide between the traditionalist and the non-traditionalist theologians of modern Catholicism, and places Daniélou unmistakably in the former category. Quite logically, therefore, the latter believes that, as long as the Jews persist in their disbelief, the church cannot abandon the duty of seeking their conversion.[59]

Like the other Catholics described in this chapter, Daniélou has devoted his personal energies to the struggle against anti-semitism in contemporary culture. In this respect, he is beyond reproach. Such, however, is the authority of patristic dogma in Catholic teaching that even a scholar of his stature is still ruled by ancient presuppositions, leaving the new wine without new wineskins in exactly the same way as Judant, Journet and Maritain.

Another great figure in post-Auschwitz Catholicism who must also be numbered among the traditionalists is Augustin Cardinal Bea. A deep regret is unavoidable in forming this conclusion, for Bea played a hero's role in the promulgation of the Vatican declaration in 1965. To liberals everywhere, not just in Catholic circles, he symbolized more than any other single person (except Pope John XXIII) the revitalized conscience of Catholic Christianity in the face of modern and historic anti-semitism. Yet, in his book-length explication of the final draft of the *Declaration on the Relation of the Church to Non-Christian Religions,* Bea reveals a surprising attachment to conservative assumptions. For one thing, he cannot completely rid himself of the deicide concept which his schema presumably sought to expunge. Thus, taking for granted that Jesus understood his relationship with God in a complete Chalcedonian sense, he writes: "Objectively speaking, there is no doubt that the condemnation and crucifixion of Christ constitutes the crime of deicide, since according to Christian teaching Jesus was man-God."[60] The stigma, conse-

59. Ibid., p. 70.
60. Augustin Cardinal Bea, *The Church and the Jewish People, A*

quently, can only be erased by claiming ignorance on the part of the Jews concerning the identity of Jesus, but their ignorance was not a total ignorance, only a "certain ignorance."[61] A measure of excuse can be found for the reluctance of the Jewish people to acknowledge Christ as "man-God," owing to the restraints of rabbinic monotheism, but, in the end, some guilt lingers as well. "There would have been no need for Christ's demand for pardon [on the cross] had their ignorance been complete and their guilt consequently excluded."[62] In other words, according to Bea, the deicide charge, with its age-old refrain, has some truth in it after all! From his lips, such a vindication is strange.

Bea, of course, does not indict all Jews, past and present. Rather, on the basis of apostolic evidence, he indicts the "perverse generation" which was centered in the city of Jerusalem during the lifetime of Christ.[63] Moreover, the perverse generation is enlarged to include Gentiles as well as Jews, Pilate as well as Herod.[64] Still, after the patristic pattern, Bea sees the destruction of Jerusalem in 70 A.D. as an act of divine judgment; the Roman treatment of the city "represents a verdict passed on moral and religious evil: stubborn pride, revolt against truth and the leading of a wicked life."[65] In spite of the manner in which he narrows down the culpability of Judaism, it is hard to discern in his book a real departure from the traditional approach to the subject. At best, the old wineskins are merely repatched in a place or two.

Even following the recent Vatican Council, therefore, the

Commentary on the Second Vatican Council's Declaration on the Relation of the Church to Non-Christian Religions, trans. by Philip Loretz, S.J., London, 1966, pps. 68–69.
61. *Ibid.,* p. 70.
62. *Ibid.*
63. *Ibid.,* p. 78.
64. *Ibid.,* p. 80 (Acts 4:24–28).
65. *Ibid.,* p. 82.

traditionalist spirit is by no means dead. Perhaps it is still dominant. Certainly, conservative theology remains a virile force in a church feeling very strongly the winds of change. That lesson should be clear.

To criticize the type of doctrine analyzed in this chapter seems, at this point, almost an anti-climactic exercise. Nonetheless, some concluding remarks are in order. Quite obviously, in light of the organic connection between anti-semitism and traditional Christian teaching, all of the above theologians are inadequate in a post-Auschwitz age. Take, for example (because he is the most original), Maritain. What responsible person can regard seriously a thinker who deduces from the supposed penchant shown by Jews for finance and commerce a metaphysical principle premised on a Jewish choice of the world over God? Simple historical pressures, namely, the social and economic role imposed on the Jews during the Middle Ages, account for Jewish progress in these realms, if a reason is required.[66] It seems, moreover, curiously perverse on the part of a Christian to dignify a Jewish "love for money" in theological terms, when this slander has constituted an excuse for the deeds of countless anti-semites, and equipped the arsenal of anti-Jewish propaganda with a potent weapon. As a metaphysician, Maritain deals irresponsibly with the contingencies of history. It is not surprising that, in the same context, he shows great blindness concerning the guilt of the church with respect to the genesis of twentieth-century anti-semitism.[67]

The trouble has two facets. As we have stressed, too much

66. For example, the fact that the Jew, as a permanent alien in medieval Christendom, was excluded from the respectable occupations and could only justify his presence by assuming the less respectable role of money-lender.
See Cecil Roth's article, "The Jew in the Middle Ages," *The Cambridge Mediaeval History,* Cambridge, Vol. VII, pps. 643–644.
67. Maritain, "The Mystery of Israel," *op. cit.,* p. 173.
Maritain finds himself unable to blame the "Church herself" for the excesses of her children.

theological anti-Judaism lies embedded in Catholic tradition to begin with. Beyond this handicap, however, Catholic ideology itself tends to pose a deeper problem. Questions of revealed truth are interwoven with the church's guardianship of the faith, so that a certain aura of absolutism hangs over its official theology about any matter (although there are now signs that this syndrome of infallibility is breaking down). Being traditionalist in their orientation in any case, the theologians described in this chapter assume uncritically that, once the "truth"—meaning the truth of dogma—is established concerning the Jews, an equilibrium between truth and charity (or love) will be no problem. That, perhaps, is the Achilles' heel of every conservative position.

If, in ultimate measure, the church held in its grasp that elusive mystery called truth, such an equilibrium would be possible, for no one could know perfect truth without doing it. But a Protestant critic cannot help but recall Reinhold Niebuhr's "paradox of grace." In his Gifford Lectures (*The Nature and Destiny of Man*), Niebuhr warns Christians against claiming to possess the truth in too unconditional a sense. "Christian history is filled not only with all kinds of pretensions that Christians stand completely beyond the egoistic corruption of the truth; it also contains, partly as a reaction to these pretensions, forms of awareness, in varying degrees of explicitness, that 'redemption' in the realm of culture and truth is a having and a not-having of the truth; and that the pretension of having it leads to a new lie. . . . The truth, as it is contained in the Christian revelation, includes the recognition that it is neither possible for man to know the truth fully nor to avoid the error of pretending that he does."[68]

The application of this warning to the present subject is obvious. In this connection it is also worth calling to mind a similar warning uttered by Nicholas Berdyaev against the objectiviza-

68. Reinhold Niebuhr, *The Nature and Destiny of Man,* New York, 1953, Vol. II, p. 217.

tion of dogma. To Berdyaev, religious insights transformed into ecclesiastical dogmas were responsible for Christian anti-semitism;[69] instead, "If the relentless struggle for Christ so demands, doctrines hitherto established and accepted must be repudiated and discarded."[70] Claiming to know too much concerning the eternal decrees of God means, in the end, to lapse into a kind of spiritual slavery in which the believer really knows nothing at all.

There is, moreover, a danger in any subordination of ethics to dogma that must not be overlooked. When, for example, a theologian as conservative as Judant insists that charity *depends* on a correct apprehension of sound doctrine, and then proceeds to define the latter in rigid patristic terms, the contradiction between "truth" and charity is apparent to everyone except the apologist herself. It is useless to oppose anti-semitism if the logic of one's private belief implies a prejudicial image of Judaism. As we have already mentioned, the failure of the German church to act in a loving spirit during the Nazi regime has provided this generation with the only demonstration it needs of the power of dogma over ethics, when the former is permitted to reign unchecked. The church would do better if its priorities were reversed.

Catholicism, in summary, cannot hope to break new ground as long its theology remains wedded, however slightly, to patristic ideas. For the fathers made no effort to understand the Judaism of their age on its terms, and certainly none to recognize in the synagogue an authentic, if non-Christian, form of biblical religion. Nor can any modern theologian who remains enclosed within the circle of tradition possibly see Judaism in this light. The old wineskins cannot suffice. The new wine, flowing in the consciousness of post-Auschwitz theologians, must seek more suitable wineskins for its ferment.

69. Nicolas Berdyaev, *Christianity and Anti-Semitism,* trans. by Alan A. Spears and Victor B. Kanter, Aldington, 1952, pps. 42f. I am paraphrasing the brief commentary on Berdyaev by Alan Spears.
70. *Ibid.,* p. 47 (Spears).

90

V. Catholic Theology in Evolution

(2) *The Radicals*

While the traditionalists occupy a more prominent place in the
Catholic world, other voices have also made themselves audible.
Mostly, these are relatively minor voices, and the chord which they
have struck remains a lesser *leitmotiv* in contemporary Catholic
theology. Nevertheless, their influence is not to be depreciated
on that account. The radical theologians are important, not
alone for their ideas, but especially for the daring with which,
as Catholic dogmatists, they have emancipated Christianity from
its own tradition, and sought a new beginning as far as a Christian understanding of Judaism is concerned. The old wineskins,
inherited from the patristic age, are cast aside. Their collective
insight is the realization that the church cannot afford the luxury
of echoing tainted doctrines in a post-Auschwitz world. The
reality of anti-semitism gives Catholicism no choice but to recast
the "truth" of its faith.

According to Renate Maria Heydenreich,[1] the first radical

1. Renate Maria Heydenreich, *Das Gespaltene Gottesvolk,* Im Auftrag der Arbeitsgemeinschaft Juden und Christen beim Deutschen
Evangelischen Kirchentag, Berlin, 1966, p. 223.

voice was that of a Belgian monk, Dom N. Oehmen, who published an extraordinary article entitled "La schisme dans le cadre de l'économie divine" in the French-language journal *Irénikon,* in 1948. (Whether the ideas expressed in this article originated with Oehmen is a matter of doubt. The independent studies of a Protestant scholar, Jean Louis Leuba, published about the same time, suggests some cross-fertilization between Protestant and Catholic thought, which subsequent similarities confirm.[2] Oehmen, however, provides a convenient place to begin.)

To this writer, the theological axiom that the Jews have been summarily ejected from the sphere of God's saving activity in historical time since the resurrection as a consequence of their refusal to enter the church is neither biblical nor true. The fathers were wrong. "Her disbelief definitely seemed to cost [Israel], through a catastrophe without equal, her special position among the peoples; after [Israel's] rejection, God created a new people in the midst of the nations; alongside of the Greeks and Scythians, the small number of believers of Israel seemingly extracted from that which had been hitherto the people of God formed with the pagans the new people of God. But this view implies too abrupt a rupture in the plan of salvation at the moment when the Christ, center of all history, was bound to assure the cohesion and continuity of events. It does not conform at all to the vision of the prophets concerning the durable importance of Israel as the eternal people of God."[3]

Instead of the traditional image of a derelict and degenerate Judaism, Oehmen posits the idea of a "schism" in the fabric of election, so that the one people of God now exist in two sundered parts: "the believing part, the church, and the unbelieving part,

2. Karl Thieme cites Leuba as an influence on his own thought in "Der oekumenische Aspekt der christlichjuedischen Begegnung," *Freiburger Rundbrief* (VIII/Nov. 1955/Summer 29/32), p. 11.
3. Dom N. Oehmen, "Le schisme dans le cadre de l'économie divine," *Irénikon* (Tome XXI/1948/1er trimestre), p. 9. My translation.

the Jews."[4] In no sense are the latter any less "elect" today than they were prior to the birth of Christianity. Moreover, to Oehmen, and contrary to the fathers, both sections of the schismatic people are subject to the same historical destiny. The Jews are not singled out for punishment. "Israel and the church go together through the world . . . Israel and the church go side by side throughout history. . . . Such is the particular situation of their schism."[5] No negative lessons or pejorative conclusions can legitimately be drawn from the Jewish dispersion, or the catastrophe of 70 A.D. If God has safeguarded the Jews, he has done so for reasons of love and grace in keeping with the covenantal relationship established at Mount Sinai, and fully valid in the twentieth century. Although outwardly divided, Christians and Jews, because of their common election, are inwardly united by a mysterious spiritual bond.

The same position was expounded by a better known French theologian, Paul Démann, whose critical examination of traditional religious teaching, *La Catéchèse chrétienne et le Peuple de la Bible,* appeared in 1952. Démann, in his investigations, notes (in Catholic catechetics) "the unfortunate habit of locating a complete rupture between Israel and the church, and imagining a *succession,* a substitution pure and simple between *two* peoples of God, an *old* and a *new.*"[6] In doing this, Christians are guilty of essentially a Marcionite ideology, with all the intellectual and spiritual dangers concealed in such a stance.[7] The more Christianity has detached its faith from its Jewish origins, the deeper its own ecclesiastical divisions and schisms have become. This patristic Hellenization of the biblical vision of history, in Démann's view, has afflicted the Christian mind with

4. *Ibid.,* p. 14. My translation.
5. *Ibid.,* pps. 14–15. My translation.
6. Paul Démann, "Israel et l'Unité de l'Église," *Cahiers Sioniens* (VIIe Année/No. 1/Mars 1953), p. 9. My translation.
7. *Ibid.*

93

a strange anti-Jewish paranoia from which the church, to its own detriment, still suffers.

Both Oehmen and Démann arrived at their theological insights through a radical rediscovery of the Pauline message in Romans 9–11 (this remarkable passage of scripture is the text for the same biblical critique of the fathers in Protestant theology as well, as we shall see in the next chapter). Démann bases his doctrine on the dialectical subtleties of Paul. "What, then, is the condition and meaning of Israel, separated from the Church? Israel, St. Paul replies, is neither entirely nor finally in disgrace: 'God has not disowned his people' (Rom. 11:2). 'In the preaching of the gospel, God rejects them, . . . but in his elective purpose he still welcomes them, for the sake of their fathers [that is, the patriarchs]; God does not repent of the gifts he makes, or of the calls he issues' (Rom. 11:28–9). 'Some, to be sure, showed unfaithfulness on their side, but can we suppose that unfaithfulness on their side will dispense God from his promises?' (Rom. 3:3)."[8]

It cannot be claimed, of course, that these chapters are in any sense the exclusive property of the radical theologians, since the traditionalists (for example, Journet) also claim Pauline authority for much more conventional theological conclusions. Indeed, as Jacqueline Plantié has remarked, Catholics in general, after Auschwitz, are "reading more frequently St. Paul's Epistles," especially Romans 9–11.[9] But the radicals claim to have uncovered Paul's real point in this tortuous analysis of God's plan in history: a point that an anti-semitic church missed in centuries of biblical interpretation. Thus, to Démann, Romans 9–11 are pivotal New Testament chapters for contemporary theology; they provide the exegetical foundations for the schism doctrine

8. Démann, *Judaism,* trans. by P. J. Hepburne-Scott, New York, 1961, p. 19.
9. Jacqueline Plantié, "The Rediscovery of Israel in Contemporary Catholicism," *The Ecumenical Review* (Vol. VII/April 1955/No. 3), p. 240.

and its ramifications for Jewish-Christian relations in the twentieth century. To read them correctly is to see the latter problem in a revolutionary new light. That, at least, is Démann's thesis; whether or not such a kerygmatizing of Romans 9–11 really produces completely salutary results, however, is a critical question which must be considered later in this chapter.

A third theologian whose viewpoint reflects the schism doctrine is the German Catholic writer, Karl Thieme. To Thieme, the basis of a Jewish-Christian entente in an ecumenical age lies in the serious application of this doctrine to every possible dimension of their mutual encounter. "It seems to us that one of the most urgent contemporary responsibilities of any Catholic theology which is to be not only conclusive and distinctive, but really nourished on the word of God, is to develop the as yet unforeseeable riches of perception which these first biblical-theological hints of Leuba and Oehmen foreshadow."[10] The schism between the church and the synagogue must be understood in its true historical context as neither the first nor the last schism in salvation history. It was preceded by the split between the northern and southern kingdoms in the Old Testament—a prototype of future schisms—and succeeded by a series of splits within Christendom itself: the eastern and western churches, the Protestant and Catholic churches, and so forth. Each schism, moreover, has damaged the spirituality of the elect people, producing many forms of alienation which continue to plague Christian unity. But the breaking apart of the church and the synagogue was the most disastrous of these divisions. For this reason, the encounter of Christians and Jews today has the strange pathos of a meeting between estranged members of the same family after a great lapse of time. Only dimly do they perceive in each other the once close brother or sister of the past. No other encounter between the great religions has this character.

Without exception, because of this unique relationship, the

10. Thieme, *op. cit.* My translation.

radical theologians stress the concept of ecumenicity. Not only does the Jewish-Christian encounter have an ecumenical character, but, instead of belonging to the periphery of the ecumenical movement, the "Jewish question" appears in their theology as the ecumenical question par excellence. This thesis is developed as follows: the church, as Thieme says, after its great schism with the synagogue, collapsed into a state of structural disorder which carried with it many fragmentations of the mind and spirit of Christianity. Some of these are illustrated by another Catholic radical, Heinrich Spaemann. To Spaemann, each of the three main segments of the Christian world—Eastern Orthodoxy, Roman Catholicism and Protestantism—embodies a defective faith.[11] In differing ways, they have betrayed the "Jewishness" of Christianity. One only has to glance at their treatment of the biblical heritage in order to confirm this indictment. Eastern Orthodoxy, with its special fondness for the wisdom literature of Israel, is unbalanced by an excessive Hellenism which colors its whole religious style. Roman Catholicism, with its special reverence for the historical and legal tradition, reveals a Latin bias which likewise colors its religious style. Protestantism, with its special prophetic *élan,* suffers also from a lack of balance in its religious style, usually in terms of an excessive individualism. Thus, declares Spaemann, one finds in each church a loss of spiritual wholeness which inevitably ends in some form of anti-Judaism.

A healing of these Christian schisms would obviously help to heal this sickness. But, in Spaemann's view, the Christian community will never achieve its true health as long as the great schism in salvation history between the church and the synagogue remains unresolved. How can John, Peter and Paul (the apostolic symbols of the three ecclesiastical traditions) dwell in genuine unity unless they are returned to their true Jewish

11. Heinrich Spaemann, "Gnadenaustausch zwischen Alt- und Neubundlichem Gottesvolk," *Das Gespaltene Gottesvolk,* pps. 261–262.

orbit?[12] The cancer of Gentilization must first of all be cured. This means of necessity an ecumenical fusion—organic as well as spiritual—with the living representatives of the other part of the schismatic people of God: the Jews. Without such a fusion, neither a unified Gentile church, nor, for that matter, an Israel locked outside the "church of Jews and Gentiles," can fully personify and perform the redemptive work of God. Only a people of God whose covenantal unity is as seamless as the robe of Christ will be equal to its supernatural vocation!

Ecumenism, therefore, has a unique meaning in radical Catholic theology. What Thieme calls the "ecumenical aspect of the Christian-Jewish encounter"[13] rests on a peculiar article of faith quite different from more common definitions of the term. In some manner (presumably by means of dialogue), Christians are required to promote the cause of union with their Jewish co-religionists on the same basis that the different branches of the church seek visible union among themselves. Logically, such a union could only be consummated if, as Paul envisioned, the Jewish world *en masse* decided to reverse its historic "no" as far as the messiahship of Jesus is concerned; in other words, if it voluntarily accepted conversion to Christianity. The church, however, according to the new theologians, is not permitted any part of the old imperialistic freedom to proselytize hapless Jews at whim; this approach was misplaced from the beginning, and remains abhorrent to the Christian conscience today. Rather, an ecumenical decision in the form of a collective recognition on the part of the synagogue of its true home in the "church of Jews and Gentiles" is their hope. Unless this spontaneous recognition occurs, the ecumenical movement, whether Catholic or Protestant, is destined to frustration and incompleteness for all time. Such is the inescapable logic of the schism doctrine.

A further aspect of this doctrine is developed by Thieme. As

12. *Ibid.*
13. Thieme, *op. cit.*

a step toward reconciliation, the latter suggests that Christians consider a modern diaconate to the Jews as a "tangible expression of thankfulness for [Gentile] participation in the spiritual inheritance of the old Israel."[14] Thieme bases this idea on Paul's invitation to the Roman Christians to help relieve the material plight of the mother church in Jerusalem (Romans 15:26f). Since the Gentile concern for the Jewish people during the last nineteen hundred years has seldom risen above sporadic efforts at conversion, it is time for Christians to ask themselves if, instead of missions, "the moral duty which confronts us today, in the faces of Jews who, in our midst, are already again excessively misjudged, slandered and partly persecuted, is not perhaps the demand, in which God himself addresses us through the need of this separated older brother, to resume the diaconate in a novel form, but in the same spirit as formerly: as a thankful witness to Jerusalem—in order to further a future unity, yet as an ecumenical request?"[15] The new diaconate would mean the most concrete service possible: a service in which the church would seek to protect the Jewish community from anti-semitism, and help Jews who become its victims. In other words, according to Thieme, the twentieth century requires a moral commitment from Christians to do exactly what the German church failed so conspicuously to do during the Third Reich!

Not surprisingly, the radical theologians have been criticized by Catholics of a more traditional bent. Thus, Gregory Baum (who is certainly not a reactionary himself) disapproves of Thieme's description of the Jew as the "elder brother" of the Christian and the synagogue as the "elder sister" of the church,[16] and Georges Tavard objects to the insinuation that the church is less than complete and perfect in itself; while Judaism may be

14. *Ibid.,* p. 9. My translation.
15. *Ibid.* My translation.
16. In Thieme's earlier work, *Kirche und Synagoge*, 1944. See Baum, *op. cit.,* p. 252, also pps. 263–264.

viewed as schismatic in relation to Christianity, "the proposition cannot be reversed."[17] These criticisms reveal a mild degree of conservative backlash, and should be evaluated accordingly. As one observer says,[18] Tavard's essay amounts to a defense of the traditional doctrine of the church as "One, Holy, Catholic and Apostolic," and therefore not in schism with anything. More pertinent than a reiteration of old dogmas, however, is a critique of the Catholic radicals from the perspective of anti-semitism itself, for the elimination of anti-Jewish elements in Christian belief is the criterion which they set for their own theology.

In contrast to the traditionalist theologians of the previous chapter, who seeks to preserve as much of the patristic corpus as possible, there is no doubt that here the wine of that "mysterious and inward experience: the memory of all that is oldest in us"[19] has found new wineskins able at last to bear much of its ferment. This doctrine is daring and heretical, and a true theological response to the post-Auschwitz situation. These theologians have not hesitated to face an existential crisis of conscience which, quite clearly, required the sacrifice of treasured assumptions. That is their greatness. The measure of their success is the fact that little if any trace of the obnoxious anti-Jewish ideas of traditional dogma lingers in their thought (something, incidentally, that cannot be said of their Protestant mentor, Karl Barth). Although still classified as non-believers, the Jews are no longer conceived in any sense as a quasi-deicide people, awaiting the blows of each epoch in their capacity as a "fallen church" (Journet) forced to work out its own "moral penalty" (Maritain). Nor, in Catholic radicalism, do they emerge as reluctant witnesses after

17. Georges Tavard, "Christianity and Israel: is the Church Schismatic?", *The Downside Review* (October, 1955), p. 350.
18. A. Roy Eckardt, *Elder and Younger Brothers, The Encounter of Jews and Christians,* New York, 1967, p. 77.
19. Hans Urs von Balthasar, *Martin Buber and Christianity, A Dialogue between Israel and the Church,* trans. by Alexander Dru, London and New York, 1961, p. 22.

the Augustinian model to the truth of Christianity. As the schismatic representatives of God's original people, they appear as the genuine equals of Christians, even, because of their "elder" status, acquiring a certain precedence over the Gentile half of the schism. The change is not minor.

Moreover, the substitution of an ecumenical basis for Catholic-Jewish relations represents a sharp deviation from the past, and one which clearly distinguishes the radical minority from the larger section of the Catholic world. Démann and Daniélou, two French theologians who have participated in Jewish-Christian dialogues, illustrate the contrast perfectly, for Démann rejects the presuppositions to which Daniélou clings.[20] Given such a generous doctrine, it is difficult to imagine any way in which anti-semitism could transform Christian faith into an instrument of its own intolerance, even if Eckardt is correct when he writes that "any and every idea, any and every conviction is tragically subject to the machinations of antisemitic depravity."[21]

Nonetheless, the possibilities exist, and must now be exposed. As we have noted, the scriptural basis of the doctrinal position developed by the radical theologians consists mainly of a fresh interpretation of Romans 9–11, or Paul's existential struggle to understand the mystery of Israel's repudiation of Christ within the framework of God's providential plan. In the past, a some-what "wooden" (Eckardt)[22] usage of these chapters typified Christian theology, so that, forgetting the temporal immediacy which induced the apostle to expect the parousia during his own lifetime, the church made Romans 9–11 the schematic outline for a much longer philosophy of history in which the Jews occupied the key position. Inevitably, this elongation of the

20. See Paul Démann, "Kirche und Israel in oekumenischer Sicht, Katholische Besinnung auf Israel seit 1945," *Christen und Juden, Ihr Gegenueber von Apostelkonzil bis heute*, Mainz, 1961, pps. 270–283.
21. Eckardt, "The Theology of Antisemitism," *Religion in Life* (Vol. XXXI/Autumn 1962/no. 4), p. 560.
22. Eckardt, *Elder and Younger Brothers*, p. 79.

time scheme tended to diminish in the Christian mind the impact of Paul's affection for his "kinsmen by race," as well as his sense of their imminent salvation, resulting in an abstract view of Judaism as something worth preserving only for the sake of the last days. Hence, a vacuum was created into which other motifs of a decidedly non-Pauline character could easily be inserted. It is not hard to imagine what these motifs were. Even Romans 9–11, in this fashion, could be made to serve the cause of anti-semitism.

The Catholic radicals, of course, as well as their Protestant counterparts, are responsible for recapturing the favorable aspects of Paul's description of the Jews such as eluded the patristic and medieval theologians. Their interpretation of Romans 9–11 does not suffer from the kind of woodenness just described. We have already cited Démann's exposition of these chapters, emphasizing the continuing election of the post-resurrection synagogue. Also noteworthy is Thieme's study of Romans 9–11 (found in the German Catholic publication, *Freiburger Rundbrief*).[23] Other examples abound. A new Jew emerges in the new exegesis: a Jew who stands first in the order of God's choice; who, like the olive tree, sustains the (Gentile) branches grafted to its stem; who, in spite of his disbelief, is still the recipient of God's love; who, in a way no Gentile ever can, represents this love to the world; who, as far as salvation is concerned, is just as secure as any Christian. Thus, with the substitution of this new theological Jew for the old Jew of Christian dogma—a Jew whose existence was only justified because, in the present, he testified despite himself to the superiority of Christian faith, and, in the future, he had a necessary role to play in the final drama—the original spirit of Romans 9–11 has apparently been recovered. But does this recovery guarantee a

23. Thieme, "Das Mysterium Israels, Gottes Wort ueber die Juden in Pauli Roemerbrief," *Freiburger Rundbrief* (Dezember 1949/Nummer 5/6), pps. 8–13; also *FR* (April, 1950/Nummer 7), pps. 9–14.

Christianity free from the "machinations of antisemitic depravity"? Unfortunately, despite the best intentions of the radical theologians, it does not.

Why? The reason is simple. Even a reborn Paulinism cannot bear the weight of an adequate and accurate modern understanding of Judaism as a religious system in the twentieth century. No Christian can see any Jew fairly through the theological prism of Romans 9–11, no matter how greatly he may empathize with Paul's passionate brotherly sentiments. Unless Judaism is understood on its own terms rather than on Christian terms (much as if the church were forced to interpret its religious meaning by means of Muslim categories), a huge gap is provided into which every form of theological prejudice can still be poured. The crux of the matter is expressed rhetorically by Gregory Baum: "Does the self-understanding of the Christian Church leave theological room for Jewish self-understanding? Or does the claim of the Church to be the people of God, the true Israel, make it impossible for Christians to acknowledge the special place which Jewish self-understanding demands."[24] If the answer to the first question is "no," then theological anti-Judaism must be regarded as an inevitability which no contemporary infusing of the church with Pauline philo-semitism can overcome.

When, moreover, Baum's question is answered vis-à-vis Romans 9–11, it has to be asknowledged that Christian self-understanding, derived from a kerygmatization of these chapters, does not and cannot allow room for "Jewish self-understanding" in any valid sense. That is the crucial and seldom noticed point. For the dominant posture in which Paul sees his fellow Jews, no matter how warm his human feelings, is essentially one of disbelief. His entire argument revolves around this enigma. (The traditionalist theologians are on sound scriptural ground when they cite the Pauline "mystery" concerning the Jews in support of their negative doc-

24. Baum, in an exchange with Arthur Gilbert in the *Journal of Ecumenical Studies* (Vol. 3/Fall 1966/No. 3), p. 552.

trine of Judaism.) Existentially, it was the failure of the great majority of the house of Israel to embrace Christianity which drove Paul to compose this section of his letter in the first place; nor, according to Johannes Munck, was the apostle alone in the primitive Christian community to be seriously troubled in this regard.[25] Yet, with Paul, the problem was especially agonizing. In his "vexed monologue," replete with "questions and answers, complaint and comfort, objections and assertions, prayers and thanksgiving,"[26] he works out an *ad hoc* solution. The providential purpose behind Israel's disbelief was to pave the way for the inclusion of the pagan world in the people of God. In spite of this divine plan, however, the Jewish refusal to enter the church was still to be deplored. Hence, although Paul's whole view places the Jews in the realm of God's special grace, what still springs into focus in the moment of writing is the Jew as a disbeliever. If one approaches Romans 9–11 in a non-dogmatic manner, remembering that the apostle in any case expected this spiritual obduracy to endure only for a few short years, this fact is unimportant. But when, after nineteen centuries of parallel development, Christians still think of Jews in terms of a kerygmatized Pauline theology, using an opinion of Judaism which, originally, was intended "not as a timeless treatment of a general problem," but as the "product of the moment,"[27] the matter assumes a much different light. Paul becomes an obscurantist.

The radical Catholic theologians are obviously not fundamentalist interpreters of scripture in the Protestant sense, but they still argue too literally from these chapters. No modern religious Jew would ever admit, or ought to admit, that Judaism as a religious faith, owes even a fragment of its spirit to a stubborn and

25. Johannes Munck, *Christ and Israel, An Interpretation of Romans 9–11,* trans. by Ingeborg Nixon, Philadelphia, 1967, pps. 14f.
26. Bent Noack, "Current and Backwater in the Epistle to the Romans," *Studia Theologica* (Vol. 19/Fasc. 1–2/1965), pps. 165–166.
27. *Ibid.,* p. 166.

blind rejection of Christian claims. Judaism does not usually define itself in relation to Christianity at all. Rather, it represents an autonomous biblical religion which has passed through many stages of growth quite independent of Christian assumptions concerning its character.[28] If recent Jewish apologists have succeeded in anything, they have certainly succeeded in clarifying this fact. Unfortunately, few Christian theologians even today have read their books in order to hear their message.

The weakness of the Catholic radicals is that they do not seem to grasp the inadequacy of Romans 9–11 as a normative definition of the Jew in relation to the Christian, even when they are otherwise well informed about Jewish beliefs and practices (for example, Démann). For the new Jew that emerges in their theology is still a non-believing Jew: a Pauline Jew rather than a real Jew. Such a Jew is necessarily artificial, and, since he lacks any true content of his own, vulnerable as well. Christians who attempt to engage in dialogue with Jews on the basis of Romans 9–11 cannot avoid in the end talking to an image without objective substance, for dialogue is impossible, as Eckardt declares, unless it means an encounter between Christians "in their faith" and Jews "in their faith."[29] It is precisely the latter that the schism doctrine does not permit, at least in its usual definition. A concept of Judaism premised on Christian kerygmatic presuppositions is not immune to the dangers of anti-semitism, for it belongs to the nature of prejudice to feed upon misconceptions, twisting them in demonic ways. After all, what did Paul know of Jewish history after the first Christian century, of Jewish religion as it has unfolded in the course of time?

A key theme of the radical theologians is that Christianity, in breaking away from Judaism, has unconsciously exposed its faith to the virus of Marcionism in ancient and modern forms, and

28. As described, for example, by Bokser, *Judaism and the Christian Predicament*. This is an elementary fact obvious to anyone with even a superficial acquaintance with the subject.
29. Eckardt, *op. cit.*, p. 66.

therefore to anti-semitism as the deadly fruit of all Marcionite doctrines. Here, as the "German Christian" movement of the 1930's demonstrates,[30] these Catholics are probably on solid ground, and it is one of the hopeful signs of modern theology that this danger has not escaped attention. If this is true, however, the critical question immediately arises as to whether every aspect of Christianity which is not genetically Jewish (the Christian faith, in Niebuhr's phrase, being an amalgam of Hebraic and Hellenistic elements)[31] should be regarded with suspicion, and depreciated accordingly. Because such a conclusion denotes a false purism, it is hardly surprising that the church has witnessed a counter-protest against its radical critics on the part of theologians who do not wish the pendulum to swing too far in an exclusively Jewish direction. Thus, Tavard writes: "When theologians and councils borrow Greek or Latin philosophical terms, they do no more than implant the Church and her Gospel in the Greek or Latin mind. This is not to say that the Church forgets her Palestinian origin to tie her destiny to Hellenic-Latin civilization."[32]

Tavard's comment finds support elsewhere. Tillich also would argue for the validity of the attempt to interpret the gospel in the language and thought-forms of the Hellenistic world, even at the risk of some distortion.[33] Judaism itself, apart from Christianity, boasted a considerable admixture of Greek elements (for example, Philo) during the centuries between the testaments. No pure strain seems to have escaped contamination by the surrounding non-Jewish culture. Where, in that case, does the danger of Marcionism begin, if an unadulterated "Jewish" Christianity is a fiction? Or, assuming that Christians must always

30. See Arthur C. Cochrane, *The Church's Confession under Hitler,* Philadelphia, 1962, chap. III.
31. Niebuhr, "The Relations of Christians and Jews in Western Civilization," *Pious and Secular America,* p. 108.
32. Tavard, *op. cit.,* pps. 354–355.
33. Paul Tillich, *Biblical Religion and the Search for Ultimate Reality,* Chicago, 1955.

acknowledge certain Hellenistic motifs in their faith, is a degree of Marcionism—and therefore anti-semitism—always latent in any Christian theology?

This question undoubtedly rests on a mistaken understanding of the problem. Marcionism, as a threat to biblical Christianity, is not a consequence of a Greek presence within the portals of the historic church in terms of religious style or theological language; rather, it is a result of a more basic spiritual disorientation affecting the intrinsic roots of Christian faith. For this reason, the antidote to Marcionism does not depend on a juggling of supposedly Jewish and supposedly Greek concepts in order to give a theological advantage to the former. A Jewish veneer to Christian thought and piety will save the church from nothing. (This, incidentally, is a popular trend in some forms of recent theological discussion, but its validity is dubious.[34]) To the extent that the Catholic radicals support such a view, one must choose sides with Tavard and Tillich. Nor, equally, does the antidote to Marcionism depend on the hope of healing the Jewish-Christian "schism" through a fusion of Jews and Christians in some form of ecumenical union designed to bring the former inside the same organic family as the Christian churches. Here, the radicals are not only unrealistic, but plainly wrong. Surely more significant, as far as the liquidation of anti-semitism is concerned, is their best insight: a rediscovery, on the part of the church, of its original and essential spiritual foundations in Judaism—in other words, a profound recapturing of its Jewish genius and Jewish soul. The loss of the Jewish essence of Christian faith is the fundamental disorder that must be corrected. To what degree can contemporary Christians think of themselves as still being, on a deep level, honorary "Jews" by virtue of their biblical lineage? That is the true question. Whether, after centuries of persecution, real Jews will prove willing to accept Christians in this capacity is another

34. For example, the present theological love affair with Jewish eschatology in the various expressions of the "theology of hope."

matter. But Pius XI was more correct than he realized in uttering the words, "Through Christ and in Christ, we are the spiritual offspring of Abraham. . . . Spiritually we are Semites."[35]

The tragedy, as we have observed, lies in the length of time that it has taken modern Christians, especially theologians, to grasp the ramifications of this simple declaration. In this and the preceding chapter, we have traced some part of the painful metamorphosis of the last three decades. In spite of the rather artificial way in which the most advanced Catholic theologians have sought to wean Christian thought away from anti-Jewish influences, at least their goal has not been wrong. Religiously, Christians and Jews belong together. A Christianity that remembers its intrinsic Jewishness as they suggest is unlikely to exalt its non-Jewish side at the expense of the "root and sap" which sustain the inner fibre of its faith. In his dialogue with Martin Buber, the Catholic Hans Urs von Balthasar (also with radical affinities) claims rightly for the Christian the same intuitive religious trust that dates back to Abraham, and which remains the oldest memory of both synagogue and church: "In prayer and contemplation, the Christian soul can feel what the Jewish soul felt . . . the memory of all that is oldest in us, and to which we remain related, that rises up within us, and is nothing else but the faith of Abraham which St. Paul and Buber speak of in a curiously dissonant harmony."[36]

A church that consciously nurtures this memory is surely immune to Marcionism in any form. Moreover as the Protestant theologian James Smart has written, Christians, when tempted by less strenuous paths of religion, can always be jolted into a state of total recall by that "rude, abrupt Hebrew guardian" of their faith, the Old Testament.[37]

35. *La Croix,* no. 17060, September 17, 1938.
36. Von Balthasar, *op. cit.*
37. James D. Smart, *The Interpretation of Scripture,* Philadelphia, p. 76.

VI. Protestantism: A Mind Divided

(1) Karl Barth

Contemporary Protestants, in common with Catholic Christians, have been driven by the pangs of an uneasy conscience toward a new personal and theological interest in Jews and Judaism. Primarily, as one would expect, the awakening has occurred in Germany, but, in a diluted fashion, it has also spread elsewhere. In North America, the beginnings are evident in some recent studies, more sociological than theological, which have demonstrated the role of pejorative religious teachings in anti-semitic attitudes still prevalent among average American Protestants.[1] Thus, glimmerings of a moral renaissance can be discerned on the horizon. But Europe remains the real center of ferment and change.

Protestantism, it must be confessed, leaves as much to be

1. For example, Charles Y. Glock and Rodney Stark, *Christian Beliefs and Anti-Semitism*, New York, 1966, pps. 73–74.
". . . it is apparent that images of the contemporary Jew as unrepentant and still guilty of the Crucifixion are not to be shrugged off as the mad notions of insignificant hate merchants. On the contrary, sizable minorities in Christian congregations embrace such beliefs about Jews, and indeed, about half at least consider it possible that such statements about Jews are accurate."

desired in its traditional doctrinal approach to Judaism as Catholic theology. Anti-semitism in pre-Auschwitz Protestant thought is extremely easy to document, requiring only the briefest of historical résumés. John Calvin, for example, reflected the characteristic religious disdain of his age toward the Jews, judging from his scattered remarks on the subject; in comparison with Luther, he must be deemed a moderate.[2] Nevertheless, Calvinism cannot escape censure, for the Calvinist doctrine of predestination provided a "spiritual climate" conducive to the idea of malediction, and this, according to Démann, "is much more important . . . than the truculent invective hurled by Luther against the Jews."[3] The point, however, is debatable. Luther's intemperate abuse in his vicious pamphlet, *Von der Juden und ihre Luegen,* published in 1543, shows the reformer in his worst light, and, probably justly, has earned him the unsavory compliment of anticipating Hitler. "Patience, Luther, Hitler will come. Your wishes will be granted, and more than granted! Recognize here the bonds of kinship, of blood, which unite the two great Germans, and place Luther where he belongs, in the first rank of the Christian precursors [of Auschwitz]."[4] The fact that the younger Luther held more kindly views on the Jewish question does not excuse his later tirade,[5] for the influence of his extreme

2. Calvin actually said little on the subject. Even his exultation at Jewish misfortunes as a fitting reward for their spiritual obstinacy is restrained in comparison with Luther: ". . . le réformateur conclut: 'meretur eorum perdita obstinatio et indomabilis, ut immensa miseriarum congerie sine fine et modo oppressi, omnes exhilarent suis malis, nemo autem eorum misereatur.' "
Cited by Jacques Courvoisier, "Calvin et les Juifs," *Judaica, Beitraege zum Verstandnis des Judischen Schicksals in Vergangenheit und Gegenwart* (Zurich, Heft 1–4, 1946), p. 206.
3. Paul Démann, "Les Juifs sont-ils maudits?", *Cahiers Sionens* (2e Année /No. 4/1er Juillet, 1948), pps. 285–286. My translation.
4. Jules Isaac, *Jésus et Israel,* p. 368. My translation.
5. In his pamphlet, *Dass Jesus Christus ein geborener Jude sei,* published in 1523, Luther sounded a moderate note quite uncharacteristic of his age. Some contemporary Jews actually hailed his writing as the dawn of a new era in Christian-Jewish understanding.

phase has far outweighed the influence of his moderate phase on the subsequent course of German Christianity. One may assign Luther's hardness of heart to the frustration of his missionary hopes concerning the Jews, as Stoehr does,[6] but the blot on the Lutheran Reformation is ineradicable; only the fact that he could not have known the future provides any semblance of extenuation. The downward spiral had begun.

One illustration from the German pulpit in the twentieth century is sufficient to reveal how tainted with anti-semitism Lutheranism had become. It is hard to believe that the following words were uttered by Martin Niemoeller, a hero of the anti-Nazi resistance. "Today is the tenth Sunday after Trinity, a day which has for centuries been dedicated in the Christian world to the memory of the destruction of Jerusalem and the fate of the Jewish people: and the gospel lessons of this Sunday throw a light upon the dark and sinister history of this people which can neither live nor die because it is under a curse which forbids it to do either. . . . Even Cain receives God's mark, that no one may kill him; and Jesus' command 'Love your enemies!' leaves no room for exception. But we cannot change the fact that until the end of its days the Jewish people must go its way under the burden which Jesus' decree has laid upon it: 'Behold, your house is left unto you desolate. For I say unto you, Ye shall not see me henceforth till ye shall say, Blessed is he that cometh in the name of the Lord!' "[7]

Many other examples abound. The uncompromising nature of this theological anti-Judaism is all the more remarkable when one recalls that classical Protestantism, with its distrust of religious authority vested in the temporal church, has never sanctified tradition in the same way as Roman Catholicism. It reveals that a dogmatic biblicism is just as dangerous as a dogmatic

6. Martin Stoehr, "Martin Luther und die Juden," *Christen und Juden,* pps. 115–140.
7. Martin Niemoeller, *Here Stand I!,* trans. by Jane Lymburn, Chicago, 1937, p. 195.

110

traditionalism. Therefore, until the post-Auschwitz era, Protestants in Germany (including many liberals) revealed as little inclination as Catholics to question the theological assumptions of patristic and medieval Christianity concerning the Jewish people and their religion. One only has to remember the extraordinary anti-semitism into which even great Protestant biblical scholars such as Emanuel Hirsch and Rudolf Kittel permitted themselves to descend in order to realize the depth of debasement to which German Protestantism was capable of sinking.[8] Otto Piper's theological study, *God in History,* published on the eve of Auschwitz (1939), exemplifies perfectly the perils of biblicism in Protestant doctrine, for in no personal sense was Piper an anti-semite or sympathetic to Nazism. On the contrary, he was an academic refugee from Hitler.

Piper begins his work with a thoroughly literal idea of "holy history" (his phrase for *Heilsgeschichte,* usually translated as "salvation history"), which, on the basis of New Testament anti-Judaism, quickly betrays him into a description of the Jews no different from the prejudiced theology of the early Christian fathers. "The modern Jew suffers with his ancestors because he shares their attitude towards Jesus. . . . The rejection of Jesus Christ is their basic sin, because their own Bible testifies of Him. . . . In the temporal realm they have been deprived of their country and dispersed over all the world; they are despised and disliked by the nations; and in the spiritual realm they have lost their leadership in holy history."[9]

An anti-Jewish biblicist mentality is by no means the sole property of German Protestants, however; much more deplorable, because his book was written long after Auschwitz, is the extremely unpersuasive attempt of the American theologian, James Daane, to defend conservative Protestant doctrines against

8. Emanuel Hirsch, *Das Alte Testament und die Predigt des Evangeliums;* Rudolf Kittel, *Theologisches Worterbuch zum Neuen Testament.*

9. Otto Piper, *God in History,* New York, 1939, pps. 95–96.

the criticisms of Jules Isaac. Daane dislikes Isaac's indictment of traditional Christian ideas concerning the Jews. "Isaac . . . is not willing to honor the Church's respect for her New Testament writings. He insists that the New Testament Gospel writers distorted the story of the crucifixion by placing the major blame upon the Jews and a minimum blame upon the Romans who, according to Isaac, were in fact chiefly responsible for Jesus' death. . . . According to the New Testament records, Jews desired, plotted, and promoted the execution of Jesus . . . No rewriting of history by those interested in freeing the Jews from responsibility for the crucifixion, or by script writers of modern movies, dispels these claims of the New Testament historical records."[10] Nor does Daane wish to abandon the old patristic dogmas concerning the fall of Judaea. "The Christian Church believes that Scripture affords sufficient grounds for regarding the destruction of Jerusalem as an act of divine judgment."[11]

Here, obviously, is a Christian who has learned little. Not only Isaac, but such scholars as Solomon Zeitlin and Paul Winter have produced penetrating historical investigations of the crucifixion with conclusions similar to those of this French critic of the New Testament.[12] Daane, of course, does not want to be considered an anti-semite. He cannot, however, really avoid the charge, for anti-Judaism is inherent in any ideology which regards the New Testament as sacrosanct after the fashion of Protestant biblicism. Hence, one is not surprised at the shrillness of his defense of traditional ideas: the integrity of scripture seems at stake. Perhaps, in the end, Catholic traditionalism is a lesser evil, for the latter is at least permitted to evolve. Protestant biblicism is fixed for all time.

After Auschwitz, the Protestant churches, by and large, also

10. James Daane, *The Anatomy of Anti-Semitism and Other Essays on Religion and Race,* Grand Rapids, 1965, p. 21.
11. *Ibid.,* p. 35.
12. Solomon Zeitlin, *Who Crucified Jesus?,* New York, 1964; Paul Winter, *On the Trial of Jesus,* Berlin, 1961.

were weighed in the balances and found wanting. We have already spoken of their personal, human failure. No less important, because it was part of their human failure, was their theological failure. A new and better doctrine was desperately needed. It was into this breach that the great Swiss theologian, Karl Barth, stepped at a critical moment.

In an article published in 1952 in the American journal *Religion in Life,* a visiting European scholar, Maria Sulzbach, announced to Americans something that had already promoted a revolution in continental theology. "In our time," she declared, "a new Christian doctrine of the Jews has been presented which, if it is eventually accepted by the Christian world to whom it is addressed, should promote a tremendous setback to anti-semitism at its very roots."[13] Sulzbach, of course, was speaking of Barth's theological reconstruction of the meaning of Judaism from a Christian perspective. Can her claim be justified?

Barth's ideas concerning the Jews, strictly speaking, are not post-Auschwitz. The German edition of the second half-volume of his masterwork, *Kirchliche Dogmatik,* which contains his systematic statement on the subject, was published in 1942. Its content, however, must have been in germination a decade earlier. Nor, so to speak, are Barth's ideas wholly original with Barth, or even entirely Protestant in origin, for his exposition of Romans 9–11 owes a measure of inspiration to at least one Catholic exegete, Erik Peterson.[14] The similarities between

13. Maria Sulzbach, "Karl Barth and the Jews," *Religion in Life* (Vol. XXI/1952/No. 4), p. 586.
14. Erik Peterson, *Die Kirche aus Juden und Heiden,* Salzburg, 1933.
Barth also has other antecedents. According to Leonhard Goppelt, his doctrine represents a second chapter to the revival of theological interest in the Jews. "It was not Neoprotestantism . . . but the heilsgeschichtliche Lutheran theology of the last century, growing out of the 19th century awakening, which substantially contributed to the present situation in the conversation . . . [Barth's] theology of election has given orientation to many theologians who have taken up the cause of Israel since the thirties."

Barth's doctrine and that of the Catholic radicals is too marked not to suggest some cross-fertilization, so that the exact source of the "schism" concept remains obscure. Here, as elsewhere, Barth has undoubtedly spoiled the Egyptians! Yet he succeeds in stamping his version of the schism between Israel and the church with a theological signature uniquely his own by attaching this doctrine to a special christological base. Thus, his portrait of the Jew becomes an integral part of his total theological system: a fact that makes it both simple and complicated at the same time.

The exegetical foundations of Barth's doctrine rest, as might be expected, on Romans 9–11, which, like the Catholic radicals, he rediscovers as a catalyst in modern theology. Against the whole of Christian tradition, he maintains that the Jews—as seen by Paul—are exactly the same elect people of God after the resurrection as they were prior to the great Christian event. In no sense has their unique status been removed. "Thus the Word of God (Rom. 9:6) is not proved false but established by the phenomenon of the unbelieving Synagogue. According to the testimony of Scripture, God has from the first chosen, differentiated and divided Israel. He has from the beginning separated the Church and Israel, Israel and the Church. And in so doing, He has confirmed the election of Israel."[15]

Any reading of Paul that misses this insight, Barth implies, seriously fails to enter the mind of the apostle. To this point, nothing distinguishes him from Oehmen, Démann or Thieme. But Barth's doctrine has a second axis lacking in the Catholic versions of the same radical interpretation of Pauline theology. Scripture is not understood correctly unless it is read from the right perspective, and, for Barth, this means that the Christian must first grasp the fundamental character of the God whose

---

Leonhard Goppelt, "Israel and the Church in Today's Discussion and in Paul," *Lutheran World* (Vol. X/No. 4/October, 1963), p. 356.

15. Karl Barth, *Church Dogmatics,* Vol II/2, English translation, Edinburgh, 1957, p. 216.

word brought both the church and the scriptural witness into existence. This God is a free God, who utters his "yes" and his "no" freely everywhere in history, but especially in the history of Israel. As Barth unfolds his doctrine of God, he requires the Jews to play a symbolic role in the Christian revelation: a role which places them squarely in the center of the gospel kerygma. To understand this second axis properly, it is necessary to extract the substructure of Barth's view of election as an essential part of his view of God.

This involves a brief excursus. As anyone who has read the *Kirchliche Dogmatik* knows, election to Barth always means christology. Hence, the elective will of God and the saving activity of God (in Jesus Christ) are indissolubly united, so that the first can be seen only through the prism of the second. To Barth, it is of vital importance to keep this unity firmly in mind, and he is harshly critical of the historic failure of Christian theology in this regard. The typical Calvinist notion of predestination, for example, is a glaring instance of a false separation between the divine will on the one hand, and revealed grace on the other. Instead of concentrating on Jesus Christ, the word in history, the Calvinists concentrated on a *decretum absolutum* prior to and apart from Jesus Christ, and betrayed themselves into theological errors from which the reformed churches still suffer. What Barth sees himself doing is nothing less than the correction of an entire tradition in Protestant theology, drawing Protestants back to the real meaning of scripture. We must fix our attention solely and totally on Jesus Christ as both the "electing God" and the "elected man": "The will of God is Jesus Christ, and this will is known to us in the revelation of Jesus Christ. If we acknowledge this, if we seriously accept Jesus Christ as the content of this will, then we cannot seek any other will of God, either in heaven or earth, either in time or eternity."[16]

Next, two factors come into play. The first has to do with

16. Ibid., p. 157.

the dialectic between election and rejection, between the "yes" of God's mercy and the "no" of God's judgment. At least, Barth declares, the old Supralapsarian version of predestination had the merit of perceiving these two sides of the divine will: because man is sinful and lost, he cannot be elected without also suffering rejection, or receive mercy without also experiencing judgment. When, however, this dialectic is attached to a *decretum absolutum* apart from Jesus Christ, the result is a disastrous (and non-dialectical) division of mankind into two groups: the saved and the damned. When, instead, the dialectic is attached to God's redemptive word in Jesus Christ, a new and altogether different juxtaposition emerges: the "yes" of God's mercy is spoken to man (that is, all humanity), while the "no" of God's judgment is reserved for God himself. That is the meaning of the cross. "If the teachers of predestination were right when they spoke always of a duality, of election and reprobation, of predestination to salvation or perdition, to life or death, then we may say already that in the election of Jesus Christ which is the eternal will of God, God has ascribed to man the former, election, salvation and life: and to Himself he has ascribed the latter, reprobation, perdition and death."[17] The implicit universalism of Barth's doctrine is not to be overlooked.[18]

The second factor involves the elect community which Barth establishes as the "natural and historical environment"[19] of the elect man, Jesus Christ. This community is more than an ordinary aggregate of individuals. It occupies a middle place between Christ and the world, and represents the former to the latter. Consequently, it also reflects the dialectic of judgment and mercy

17. *Ibid.*, p. 163.
18. Although Barth refuses to bind the freedom of God by adopting a universalist position in so many words, the logic of his view of election implies universalism. See G. C. Berkouwer, *The Triumph of Grace in the Theology of Karl Barth*, trans. by Harry R. Boer, Grand Rapids, 1956.
19. *CD.*, p. 196.

116

as the "ecclesiological form of what we have previously described in christological terms."[20] Here, the Jews come into the system. According to Barth, the believing segment of the elect community, the church, is assigned the task of demonstrating the "good-will [*Willigkeit*], readiness [*Bereitschaft*] and honor [*Ehre*] of God," corresponding to the elected man, Jesus Christ, in his capacity as the "risen Lord of the Church."[21] Thus, the Christian community becomes the "authentic witness of the mercy in which God in choosing man for fellowship with Himself turns towards him His own glory."[22]

To the unbelieving segment of the elect community, the Jews, is assigned the opposite task of demonstrating the "unwillingness [*Unwilligkeit*], incapacity [*Unfaehigkeit*] and unworthiness [*Unwuerdigkeit*] of man with respect to the love of God directed to him," corresponding to the elected man, Jesus Christ, in his capacity as the "crucified Messiah of Israel."[23] Thus, the Jews (or the "Synagogue") become the "authentic witness of the judgment that God takes upon Himself by choosing fellowship with man."[24] Together, in other words, Christianity and Judaism comprise a polar contrast as the two sides of the elect community in which God's mercy and judgment are mirrored in a visible and tangible fashion to the world.

It may be argued that Barth has destroyed his own dialectic by once again dividing men into two distinct groups. One must remember, however, that, unlike the Supralapsarians, he is not saying that one group is saved and the other is damned. In Barth's theological vision, everyone is saved—in principle at least. Nor, like the patristic theologians, does he cast the Jews outside the sphere of salvation history. To the contrary, he regards them as the inner core of salvation history (Romans

20. *Ibid.*, p. 198.
21. *Ibid.*, p. 199.
22. *Ibid.*, p. 198.
23. *Ibid.*
24. *Ibid.*

9–11). Nevertheless, since they have perpetuated their existence without believing in Christ, they must witness despite themselves to the meaning of human life when the latter is organized in opposition to God. The Christian symbolizes man with his face turned toward God's grace; the Jew symbolizes man (the same man) with his face turned away from God's grace. But God chooses both Jews and Christians as his special people among the nations, and makes them the living personification of a moral parable so that men who are neither Jews nor Christians can discern through their presence the mysterious depths of God's mercy and judgment.

In this intricate manner, the Jewish people are made part—a conspicuous part—of the Christian kerygma. The logic of Barth's system requires their incorporation into his doctrine of election. One is tempted to wonder what he would have done had Judaism disappeared *in toto,* as Hitler desired, and another witness to God's "no" had had to be found. Since, however, Barth considered the Jews to be the only valid natural argument for the existence of God, he never admitted this possibility. "They could and can disappear just as little as God's faithfulness can come to an end."[25]

Anti-semitism, moreover, becomes part of the same numinous identity which the Bible imposes on the Jews, and which they can never shake off. "The Jew pays for the fact that he is the elect of God . . . The sun shines down—not on the Egyptians and Babylonians, not on the Philistines and Moabites, not on the Greeks and Romans, not on the English nor on the Swiss, but on the chosen people of Israel, the Jews—and thus brings to the light the truth about us all. This we suspect and therefore dislike the Jews. Therefore, we deem it necessary to punish the stranger in our midst, with contempt, scorn and hatred. The most wrong-headed thing we could do! What is the good of

25. Barth, "The Jewish Problem and the Christian Answer," *Against the Stream, Shorter Post-War Writings—1946–52,* London, 1954, p. 196.

turning the mirror to the wall, or even smashing it? That will not alter the fact that we are still what we saw ourselves to be in the mirror. However, the folly of turning the mirror to the wall and smashing it is the only bit of sense in all the nonsense of anti-semitism."[26]

To the Gentile, whose civilized veneer usually disguises idolatrous impulses deep within his soul, the sight of a Jew is an intolerable reminder that human self-sufficiency is a myth which men tell themselves in order to escape God. No one can stand facing the truth about himself daily. Auschwitz, consequently, was a desperate attempt to rid the world, not only of the Jews, but of God. That is its theological meaning.

Is this doctrine, as Sulzbach claims, "a tremendous setback to anti-semitism at its very roots? Some doubts are in order.

Like the radical theologians in rebellion against traditional Catholic dogmas, Barth begins by using Romans 9–11 kerygmatically. This means that his doctrine is subject to the limitations inherent in Paul's treatment of the topic in the context of the first Christian century, notably the exaggerated concern of the apostle with the mystery of Jewish disbelief. For Paul, this mystery was of understandable personal importance. But what of Christian theologians many centuries later? We have already taken to task Barth's Catholic counterparts for absolutizing the Pauline vision of Judaism as a timeless statement of theological truth. Barth does the same thing, but compounds the sin even further. The Jews, on the basis of their disbelief, are transformed into a living mirror of God's judgment against all human disbelief. Disbelief, in fact, is the core of their role in the Barthian system. For this reason, a critic such as Eckardt is correct in observing that, in spite of its positive features, Barth's Christian theology of the Jews is one of "discontinuity" rather than "continuity" between Judaism and Christianity.[27] In other words, he is too Pauline, or Pauline in the wrong

26. *Ibid.,* p. 199.
27. Eckardt, *op. cit.,* pps. 58f.

119

sense, imprisoning his doctrine in a theological straitjacket from which it never becomes extricated. The result, at best, is a *tour de force.*

The difficulties, moreover, do not end at this point. What are we to think of the whole manner in which the Jews are objectified in Barth's theology without any apparent reference to— or knowledge of—real flesh-and-blood Jews or real Jewish faith and religious self-understanding? Is Barth's Jew actually any less artificial and contrived than the patristic or medieval Jew of the older theologians? Does Barth's "Synagogue" bear any true resemblance to synagogues as they exist at the present time? Is it legitimate for a Christian theologian, however purely motivated, to construct a unilateral "Christian" doctrine of Judaism in order to complete the "symmetry"[28] of a theological system? Do not Barth's underlying assumptions about revelation, and its christological focus, betray him into a type of religious totalitarianism in which Jews are not permitted to know anything concerning their own identity except what they are taught at the gates of the church? Despite the immense psychological difference between Barth and his theological predecessors, are we not really halfway back in the Middle Ages if we accept his peculiar vision of Jewish existence?

Few Christians, one suspects, realize the extent to which the average Jew feels uncomfortable at being made to play a role in Christian eschatology, even when this role is not a deliberately malignant one. One exception perhaps is Tavard, who recognizes that "No man likes to become an object, even for theological reflection."[29] The danger, of course, is that, in being seen as an object, one might be seen as less than a person. To Christians, more secure in what is still a majority culture in spite of impend-

28. See R. M. Brown's Introduction to Georges Casalis, *Portrait of Karl Barth,* trans. by R. M. Brown, New York, 1963, p. 31.
29. "The Council's 'Declaration' on Non-Christians," editorial by Georges Tavard, *Journal of Ecumenical Studies* (Vol. 3/Fall 1966/ No. 3), p. 1962.

ing changes, this danger might seem more academic than real, but to Jews it has an actuality that historical experience supports. Even at those moments when medieval Christendom forgot the stigma whereby the deicide people lived an uneasy life in its midst, the Jews by and large were still less important as fellow human beings than as tolerated agents whose eventual conversion would signal the end of time. Remembering this lesson, a modern Jewish critic has written: "The pragmatic test of a philosophy is what it turns out to be when it has filtered through the minds and emotions of the mass of men, and in this respect the possibilities of 'Neo-Reformation' orthodoxy seem to have some ominous contours. Theology, whatever its special sociological or historical insights, is ultimately occupied with the relation of man to man and man to God. May not the attempt to incorporate within it, as a primary concept, the idea of 'people' or 'nation' (whatever it is that the Jews are), be the very first idolatrous act? Can there be any exception in theology to the universal identity of man that does not work to the disadvantage of man, theology and Jews?"[30]

Beyond any doubt, Barth's doctrine falls under this critique. To be sure, there is a qualitative difference between the twilight of a fallen existence and the bright daylight of life within the sphere of God's promise, but this difference does not cancel the absence of real humanity in the theological Jew of Barth's making. Once again, it will not do to project Romans 9–11 on the large canvas of post-resurrection Jewish history. Only a distorted picture can result. In the last analysis, Barth's doctrine of the Jews is prey to the same failure as his doctrine of man: everything is defined in terms of a monistic christology with one dimension alone. Because of this trait, moreover, he unwittingly misrepresents Judaism in order to heighten the contrast between Judaism and Christianity. Here, he is guilty of a perennial

30. Irving Kristol, review of Eckardt's book, *Christianity and the Children of Israel,* in *Commentary* (Vol. V/April 1948), p. 386.

weakness among theologians, namely, seeing only what one wants to see in the opposite reality. "Just as the Christian theologian, so Schweitzer has told us, has often found in the 'historical' Jesus the affirmation of his own position, so frequently has his portrayal of Judaism served as a foil for that position."[31]

In making this observation, Lou Silberman was thinking of Bultmann rather than Barth, but his statement fits the latter perfectly. For Barth's "Synagogue" possesses no more true integrity in real life than Bultmann's theological portrait of first-century Judaism in the colors of self-isolation;[32] both are surrogates for positions "within contemporary Christian theology,"[33] not encounters with objective truth. Hence, it is impossible to avoid the conclusion that Barth's view of Judaism ends in the creation of a type of theological (rather than a physical) ghetto, including all the attendant evils of ghetto existence: misunderstanding, isolation, alienation and de-humanization. No Jew would ever care to be lodged in such a place, and who can blame him? In spite of Sulzbach's glowing praise, therefore, the claim that Barth's doctrine is capable of striking a mortal blow at the roots of anti-semitism does not seem convincing. He only appears in this light when his theology is compared with the much less savory views of the fathers.

Furthermore, certain patristic echoes linger in Barth. One catches, for example, a note of Augustine in Barth's delineation of the Jewish witness to man's "unwillingness, incapacity and unworthiness" with respect to God's love, although the theme has been transposed to a less discordant key. Nonetheless, the Jews still emerge, as they have for centuries, as reluctant witnesses to the truth of the Christian faith: a role which is based on a historical lie, and which, to say the least, must be highly disconcerting to a people with a profound pride in their

31. Lou H. Silberman, "Judaism and the Christian Theologian," *The Journal of Religion* (Vol. XXXVII/October 1957/No. 4), p. 246.
32. In Bultmann's essay, *Das Urchristentum im Rahmen der Antiken Religionen*, Zurich, 1949, pps. 63–110.
33. Silberman, *op. cit.,* p. 251.

own religious heritage. Once the exegetical and christological foundations of Barth's doctrine become eroded, leaving his theological Jew as simply an image to be secularized in the popular mind, there is no reason to suppose that it will be any less vulnerable to the "influx of pagan hatred" (Baum) than the older stereotype.

An additional patristic trait which lingers in Barth is his predisposition to argue from history. Like the traditionalists, he regards Jewish survival throughout their long exile as a concomitant of their supernatural vocation. This, in his view, is not a punishment but a testimony to the supremacy of divine grace: a grace which continues to act against all the laws of human and historical probability. Although the rationale is different, the mode of the argument remains unchanged; such events as the fall of Judaea in 70 A.D., which are susceptible of more mundane explanations, have a hidden providential meaning which only faith, that is, Christian faith, can discern. In fairness, it must be acknowledged that some Jewish theologians also adopt a similar view of Jewish history, although, of course, on Jewish rather than Christian grounds.[34] Barth is not alone. Yet, the temptation to twist the vicissitudes of history in order to prove a theological point is more serious in the case of a Christian theologian, because of the abuse involved in this *modus operandi* in the Christian past. Barth lifts the patristic curse, but the logic of his doctrine nonetheless requires an interpretation of the catastrophes of Judaism in judgmental terms; otherwise, his claim that the Jews are living witnesses to the consequences of human disbelief would scarcely carry conviction. Moreover, only through the elimination of any natural reason for Jewish survival can a claim for divine grace as the operative factor in their strange continuance be made.

Thus, however differently motivated, Barth's implied argument

34. For example, Jacob Neusner, "Judaism in the Secular Age," *Journal of Ecumenical Studies* (Vol. 3/Fall 1966/No. 3), pps. 519–541.

from history veers dangerously close to the style of reasoning employed by the patristic theologians. Modern historians such as Hannah Arendt are properly scornful of non-historians who are cavalier in their use of historical data. Equally relevant is the warning of the philosopher Karl Loewith, who, recalling the arrogant self-assurance with which Christian writers from Augustine onward have detected the presence of God in specific historical events, declares: "A more modest use of providence would be less questionable and more Christian."[35]

Although too sophisticated a concept for the fathers, who did not know the term "anti-semitism" in any case, Barth's tendency to ontologize this moral and spiritual problem into something supernatural also raises questions. Once again, this is not a Barthian characteristic alone; certain Jewish thinkers (Will Herberg, for example)[36] have done the same. In addition, other Christian theologians, quite dissimilar to Barth, have been equally explicit in their feeling that anti-semitism has supernatural dimensions. We have already mentioned Tillich's description of the Jews as peculiar symbols of the "Lord of time," and, therefore, always subject to persecution at the hands of the "gods of space," incarnate in the various national and racial ideologies.[37] Unlike Tillich, however, Barth appears to incorporate anti-semitism into the structure of salvation history, so that, in effect, it becomes the other side of Jewish election: a condition as transcendental as the choice of the Jew, and totally different in kind from other forms of group prejudice or conflict. When we remember that, for Barth, to be a Jew means to symbolize (as it does not for Tillich) man's "unwillingness, incapacity and unworthiness" with respect to God's love, the onus of having to attract the malice of those who do not wish to be

35. Karl Loewith, *Meaning in History,* Chicago, 1949, p. 142.
36. Will Herberg, *Judaism and Modern Man,* New York, 1959, pps. 273–274.
37. Chapter I.

reminded of their unwillingness, incapacity and unworthiness makes the Jewish fate deeply tragic. We arrive here at what Arendt has styled "eternal antisemitism," a doctrine in which "Jew-hatred is a normal and natural reaction to which history only gives more or less opportunity."[38]

Arendt attacks this doctrine as a means of avoiding the true historical issues. But surely the attempt to enlarge anti-semitism into a metaphysical principle contains a worse danger. Because an air of fatalism surrounds the Jewish plight from beginning to end, any practical effort to mitigate this plight must labor under the handicap of certain defeat. Do the valiant campaigns of such organizations as the Anti-Defamation League to counteract anti-semitism on the empirical level in modern society have any real point? To be sure, it is better to give history less, rather than more, opportunity to murder Jews, but, if anti-semitism is as potent as Barth believes, the cause is lost anyway. Even that "less" opportunity breeds a perpetual insecurity.

For this reason, one cannot help sympathizing with Ruben-stein's despair at Christian theologians who persist in making their main appeal to providence in the face of the violence inflicted on the Jews in the present century. "The more one studies the classical utterances of Christianity on Jews and Judaism, while, at the same time, reviewing the terrible history of the Nazi period, the more one is prompted to ask whether there is something in the Christian philosophy of history, when pushed to a metaphysical extreme, that ends in the justification of, if not the incitement to, the extermination of the Jews."[39] This indictment extends beyond the teaching of contempt. It embraces exactly the kind of theological rationale concerning Auschwitz that theologians such as Barth provide. While there is merit in the latter's discernment of the perverse depths in the human

38. Hannah Arendt, *The Origins of Totalitarianism*, p. 7.
39. Richard L. Rubenstein, "Jews, Christians and Magic," *Christianity and Crisis* (Vol. XXIII/No. 7/April 30, 1962), p. 66.

soul that anti-semitism apparently stirs, must one go so far as to locate a spiritual disease in the metaphysical ordering of history in order to prove its radical evil? Such a doctrine is a matter of conjecture in any case; it can only be believed or disbelieved. If Christians choose to accept it as an article of faith, however, they should be conscious of the dangers that it entails.

Perhaps, in the end, Barth's doctrine of the Jews represents one of the least satisfactory aspects of his magnificent dogmatics. No one, of course, knowing the great personal generosity of his spirit, could ever have impugned his motives. His impassioned and early opposition to Hitler is famous, and no man would have wished less to enhance the burden that Jews have been forced to bear in modern times. One would like to accept Sulzbach's dictum that he has provided the Christian world with a theological antidote to anti-semitism, but such is not the case. In fact, when compared with the radical theologians of Catholic Christianity, his doctrine actually reveals more patristic overtones and a less revolutionary quality. Nonetheless, his voice has spoken a decisive word in continental theology. His admirers are legion, and the impetus for a total reconsideration of Christian belief in the light of Auschwitz is one of his many gifts to the church. In that sense, Christians and Jews both stand in his debt.

Barth's various Protestant imitators cannot all be dealt with in this chapter, nor is this necessary. All are identical in the one essential belief: the Jews, according to Romans 9–11, are still the elect people of God, and therefore exist in an unique spiritual/organic relationship with the church best described as a schism. Some of Barth's followers are also well-known names, such as Helmut Gollwitzer.[40] Many of the same weaknesses already criticized in Barth and the Catholic radicals who share the schism doctrine are present in Gollwitzer and other European Protestant theologians as well. In some cases, new weaknesses compound the former.

40. Helmut Gollwitzer, "Die Judenfrage—eine Christenfrage," *Christen und Juden*, pps. 289–290, and other writings.

An example is Jakob Jocz. This theologian takes Barth as his starting point, but existentializes Barth's doctrine in such a fashion as to make the church and the synagogue, instead of fixed entities, timeless symbols of the eternal struggle between grace and law within both of these religious communities and within every individual person. "To us the dividing line, though real, remains fluid: the Church is frequently Synagogue and the Synagogue is sometimes Church."[41]

It does not require much insight to see that here we are presented not only with an arbitrary use of terms, but also with a species of Christian anti-Judaism. For Jocz's value judgments are consciously slanted against the intrinsic content of Jewish faith, which, in common with many Protestants (especially continental Protestants), he apparently imagines to be legalistic. (Another great offender in this regard is the Swedish theologian Anders Nygren, who erroneously applied the motif of "nomos" to Jewish religion in his major study *Agape and Eros*.[42]) But this is the perfect example of the misinterpretation of one religion when the categories of another are imposed from the outside. Quite understandably, Jews resist the notion, derived from Pauline theology, that obedience to the Torah has any connection with spiritual justification in the Christian—and especially the Lutheran—sense. That is not its intent and motivation at all. It is a Christian presupposition that Judaism does not share which regards the human situation as a struggle between works-righteousness (law) and grace. If mankind is not trapped in the snares of original sin, it does not need the kind of redemption that Christianity offers.[43] Like Barth, and many Christians, Jocz

41. Jakob Jocz, *A Theology of Election, Israel and the Church*, London, 1949, p. 134.
42. Anders Nygren, *Agape and Eros*, trans. by Philip S. Watson, Philadelphia, 1953.
43. "To the Christian, the man who has not experienced the supernatural grace of God remains unredeemed; the career of the Christ Jesus is held to have brought salvation to previously unredeemed man. To the Jew, man was never lost in sin, and hence not in need of salvation in this sense."
Sandmel, *op. cit.*, p. 71.

creates an artificial and phony Judaism as a suitable foil for his own ideas.

Another disciple of Barth who views modern Judaism mainly through the prism of Romans 9–11 is the Scottish theologian, T. F. Torrance. Even more than Barth, Torrance seems full of patristic echoes. "Israel . . . suffered because of its persistent refusal of grace, suffering more and more until in the ultimate act of God's self-giving in the Incarnation, Israel rejected it in the crucifixion of the Messiah, and in so doing shattered itself on the Cross—theologically, the complete destruction of Jerusalem and the Temple in A.D. 70 had to follow upon the crucifixion of the Son of Man."[44]

Not content with this assertion, Torrance actually has the temerity to suggest that the deep emotional conflicts of many Jewish patients concerning the crucifixion of Jesus, which psychoanalysis (for example, Carl Jung) has uncovered, must mean that the Spirit of God is "working with Israel in a decisive way, pressing it to the point of looking upon Him whom it had pierced."[45] It is more likely that these patients are suffering from the psychic ravages inflicted by a Gentile society through the cruel misuse of Christian symbols. One finds it hard to imagine a more unfavorable exposé of the capacity of some "biblical" theologians to lose touch with reality! Fortunately, most of Barth's followers are better balanced, and not given to this kind of extremism.

The point at which the Catholic radicals and their Protestant counterparts meet most significantly is in the realm of ecumenism. Barth himself struck this note in declaring that "the modern ecumenical movement suffers more seriously from the absence of Israel than of Rome or Moscow."[46] Others have taken

44. T. F. Torrance, "Israel and the Incarnation," *Judaica* (Heft 1–4/1957), p. 7.
45. *Ibid*, p. 16.
46. Barth, *CD*, Vol. IV/3/2, p. 878, fn.

up the same cry. Fadiey Lovsky, for example, speaks critically of the World Council of Churches because of its deficient understanding of ecumenicity. "The excessive prudence of the ecumenical assembly at Evanston in 1954, when it refused to mention Israel in its message on Christian hope, not only resulted in a theological error but also a negation of its own true ecumenical task."[47]

In the same context, Hendrik Berkhof has written: "If we have some idea of the range of these two great breaches within the people of God, which testify at once to human guilt and to Divine supremacy, we are to some extent prepared to envisage the fission of the Christian community also in the proper light."[48]

More recently, there is the example of an influential study-book, *Israel und die Kirche,* issued by the Netherlands Reformed Church. "We should be able to go still one step further and see our relation to Israel in an ecumenical light, in which we consider the division between the church and Israel as the first great schism within the one body of the community of God. Israel was the cradle of ecumenism. This concept is connected so closely with the cradle of Israel that an ecumenical movement severs itself from its own origin if it does not occupy itself with its relation to this people. For, without Israel, the church cannot experience its ecumenical character in full measure."[49]

These representative statements virtually paraphrase the ecumenical credos of Démann, Thieme, Oehmen and other like-minded Catholics, and reveal how closely the two radical streams have merged in continental theology. In a later chapter, we must assess the implications of this redefinition of the meaning and

47. Lovsky, *Antisémitisme et Mystère d'Israel,* p. 510. My translation.
48. Hendrik Berkhof, "The Three Divisions in the Life of the Church," *The Ecumenical Review* (Vol. VI/Jan. 1954/No. 2), p. 143.
49. *Israel und die Kirche, Eine Studie, im Auftrag der Generalsynode der Niederlaendischen Reformierten Kirche zusammengestellt,* Zurich, 1961, p. 43. My translation.

goal of ecumenism for the Jewish-Christian encounter. At the moment, the fact that the struggle against anti-semitism has brought Catholics and Protestants together in a common religious front, albeit a minority within both church, is of great importance. Pricked by the same bad conscience, these Christian theologians have found a striking unity of purpose, transcending their usual differences. Let no one underestimate the form-changing power of a theological renaissance!

VII. Protestantism: A Mind Divided

(2) *The Liberal Impulse*

The Protestant world has other currents. A conservative biblicism or a neo-orthodox biblical theology have never been its only theological options in recent times. Unlike Roman Catholicism, which, until almost the present decade, has generally resisted an unrestrained critical exploration of scripture and dogma, the Protestant churches have suffered a profound intellectual cleavage since the dawn of higher criticism. To define the Protestant mind, therefore, is a complicated task.

The liberal side of this cleavage has passed through many phases. Today, even its latest phase, "de-mythologizing" (Bultmann), has acquired a stale ring in the rapidly changing fashions of contemporary theology. For this reason, liberalism is neither a fresh nor precise means of distinguishing one kind of Protestant worldview from another; it admits of too many variations. Ordinarily, in the late sixties, it would be dropped as a category in theological discussion (despite the neo-liberalism which seems to have succeeded neo-orthodoxy) because of this imprecision. As far as the Christian understanding of Judaism is concerned, however, the term "liberal" has not been drained of its theological relevance. A large enough dichotomy exists between the theologians described in this chapter, and those in the preceding chapter, to justify its retention in the context of this book. With an awareness of its limitations, we shall use it accordingly.

Although the belief in applying the tools of scientific criticism to the scriptures is usually regarded as the keystone of liberal Christianity, an older body of ideas antedates this essentially modern definition. What, historically, comprises religious liberalism in a Christian setting? Three emphases are important: (1) an underlying belief, dating back to the earliest Christian "liberals," Clement of Alexandria and Origen, in the efficacy of human reason as part of the universal *logos*. Man, in other words, is intended by God to use his mind freely and without inhibition, since reason links him directly to God. In a Christian setting, this belief, transmitted in secular form through the Enlightenment (eighteenth century), has found modern theological expression in an optimistic view of human nature and a progressivistic view of history. Judaism, incidentally, has traditionally shared a similar respect for reason and a similar optimism with regard to man's nature. (2) A preoccupation with ethical concerns as a central, if not exclusive, focal point of religious faith. This type of theology, which can be traced as far back as Abélard, owes its modern origins to the changes wrought in the mental landscape of religious man by Kantian philosophy, and came to full flower in the nineteenth century. Today, long after Ritschl and Rauschenbusch, Protestant liberals continue to be inspired by the biblical social image of the "kingdom of God." Judaism also has passed through a Kantian phase, and characteristically bears a deep religious sense of ethical obligation. (3) An attitude of openness to culture in all its forms, and to non-Christian religions as well. This is a more recent emphasis of liberal Christianity, although even the oldest Christian liberals have never regarded revelation as the exclusive property of the church. Judaism, needless to say, has its own tradition of religious tolerance: "Among all the nations there are just individuals, and they will have a share in the world to come."[1]

All three emphases tend to enter into a liberal Christian theology of Judaism, whether implicitly or explicitly. They vary, however, among different theologians, with the result that no two Christian liberals are exactly similar. In fact, in a Protestant spectrum, liberalism ranges all the way from unitarianism, at one pole, to the more biblically oriented exponents of neo-orthodoxy at the other. Further, in its American expression, neo-orthodoxy has always retained a strong liberal flavor lacking in its continental expression. "When I find neo-orthodoxy turning into sterile orthodoxy or a new Scholasticism," writes Reinhold Niebuhr, "I find that I am a liberal at heart, and that many of my broadsides against liberalism were indiscriminate."[2] It is not a coincidence that Niebuhr, in his attitude toward Judaism, is very much of a liberal, despite his famous depreciation of reason.

Generalizations are usually hazardous, but, in dealing with liberal Christian religious views concerning the Jews, one generalization is sound. Protestants shaped by this religious ethos, although by no means immune to anti-semitism on other levels of mind and spirit, possess an innate suspicion of dogmas inherited from the Christian past. A recent careful study, *Christian Beliefs and Anti-Semitism,* confirms the notion that hostile religious images of the Jews remain relatively uncommon in liberal congregations, whereas, in conservative congregations, they are strikingly common.[3] Non-fundamentalist Protestants simply do not think naturally in the categories of a pre-critical scriptural or doctrinal tradition. Among more unqualified liberals, dogma in any form has long been an outgrown approach to faith.

Unfortunately, however, it does not follow that a break with

1. *Tosefta,* Sanhedrin XIII.
2. See the symposium, *How My Mind Has Changed,* edited by Harold E. Fey, New York, 1961, p. 117.
3. Glock and Stark, *op. cit.,* p. 80.

patristic theology automatically ensures that Judaism, as a religious tradition, will either be understood sympathetically or treated fairly at the hands of liberal Christians. One only has to remember Friedrich Schleiermacher's theological estimate of Judaism as an inferior form of monotheism to Christianity in order to realize that a liberal Christian faith is also susceptible to prejudice. Indeed, to Schleiermacher, the Jew was as far removed as the pagan from the perfect religion (Christianity), so that "Christianity cannot in any wise be regarded as a remodeling or a renewal and continuation of Judaism."[4] Yet Schleiermacher, in many respects, remains the intellectual father and greatest theologian of liberal Protestantism.

With their difference in viewpoint, a clash between neo-orthodox and liberal Protestants on the subject of the Jews was inevitable sooner or later after the Second World War. It occurred dramatically at the second assembly of the World Council of Churches, which met in Evanston, Illinois, in 1954. "One wonders," commented the editor of *The Ecumenical Review* later, "whether anybody had foreseen that the issue which would provoke the greatest misunderstanding and the most heated discussion would be that concerning the attitude and relation of the Church to Israel."[5] Evidently no one did.

The initial dispute arose over the differing connotations attached by different delegates to the word "Israel."[6] To those from the continental churches, under the aegis of the absent Karl Barth, its significance transcended its obvious political (that is, the state of Israel) and ethnic meaning. As we have seen, in Barth's view, Israel is essentially a theological concept, embracing the Jews in a sense analogous to the concept of *ecclesia,* or

4. Friedrich Schleiermacher, *The Christian Faith,* English translation of second German edition, Edinburgh, 1928, p. 61.
5. "World Council Diary," *The Ecumenical Review* (Vol. VII/April 1955/no. 3), p. 284.
6. See W. W. Simpson, "Co-operation between Christian and Jews," *ibid.,* p. 255.

church. But to the Anglo-Saxon delegates, by and large, this use of the term was inadmissible, at least as far as contemporary Jews were concerned. After sampling typical American Protestant reactions at the Council to the continental doctrine, F. Ernest Johnson concluded: "Perhaps one may generalize to this extent: Thoughtful Protestants in America agree that the concept of Israel, the People of the Covenant, has great significance for the Church and for the Christian tradition; but many questions arise concerning the extent to which Christianity should be considered as furnishing a theological norm for the Jewish people."[7] At stake, of course, was more than a semantic quarrel about a single word; in this confrontation, a deeper theological problem inadvertently came to the surface, setting the stage for a debate within Christendom which has not yet been resolved.

The continentals, following Barth, argued from Romans 9–11, catching the liberals off guard. Only later did an American Lutheran theologian, Joseph Sittler, isolate the pertinent question. Should these chapters from Paul, he asked, properly be regarded as "illustrative" as far as the Jews are concerned, or should they be regarded as "kerygmatic"—that is, as a normative statement of Christian faith? When the apostle distinguished between "Israel after the flesh" and "Israel after the spirit," in other words, "what is the meaning of this distinction for the church as it confronts in actual historical concreteness the living representatives of the ancient people of God?"[8]

Having, in two previous chapters, already considered the kerygmatic position and some of its inherent weaknesses, it is now time for an examination of the non-kerygmatic or liberal position, with its general suspicion of all theological absolutes governing

---

7. F. Ernest Johnson, "The Jewish Question as an Ecumenical Problem," *The Ecumenical Review* (Vol. VII/October 1954–September 1955), p. 231.

8. Joseph Sittler, "The Abiding Concern of the Church for the Jewish People," *The Ecumenical Review* (Vol. VII/April 1955/no. 3), p. 223.

Jewish-Christian relations derived from the New Testament, and its particular suspicion of such a theological use of Romans 9–11. This position, as far as I am aware, has been articulated only by Protestant theologians, although some signs of the liberal impulse can be detected in a few modern Catholic writers, for example Rosemary Ruether.[9]

Auschwitz is a village in Poland, and liberal Protestant Christianity, with its "Anglo-Saxon" coloration, is mainly—though not exclusively—British and American in its genius. For this reason, perhaps, and because Great Britain and the United States opposed Germany by force of arms in the Second World War, the significance of Auschwitz as an exposure of western, rather than German, sinfulness has been slow in penetrating the American churches. Not many Americans have seen themselves disclosed as guilty participants in its fires. Anti-semitism, as a result, has not shaped post-Auschwitz Christian theology in the United States as decisively as it has in Europe. Until quite recently, it has not been considered as a matter with much theological relevance at all, although the times may now be changing. This situation undoubtedly explains the puzzlement experienced by the American delegates to Evanston, when their continental counterparts insisted so vehemently that the Jewish question was the most important theological task facing the assembly. Nothing in American "churchianity" would ever have induced such a notion. Most American Protestants are used to living in reasonable harmony with their Jewish neighbors, and, if Herberg is correct, this harmony has been mutual.[10] Consequently, the furor

9. See Rosemary Ruether, "Theological Anti-Semitism in the New Testament," *The Christian Century* (Vol. LXXXV/no. 7/February 14, 1965), pps. 191–196.
10. Will Herberg, *Protestant-Catholic-Jew, An Essay in American Religious Sociology,* New York, 1955, pps. 225–256.
Herberg contrasts Catholicism unfavorably with urban Protestantism as far as typical Jewish suspicions of Christian anti-semitism are concerned.

136

stirred up by continental Protestants has been difficult to digest.[11] Indeed, few persons in America have attempted to digest it: a fact which accounts for the paucity of "liberal" theological responses to the continental doctrine (Barth), or, for that matter, to ordinary traditional religious clichés.

There have been exceptions, however. James Parkes is one. Reinhold Niebuhr is a second, and, most recently, the name of A. Roy Eckardt must be added, although, like Niebuhr, Eckardt has neo-orthodox affinities as well. While Paul Tillich's comments on Judaism scarcely occupy a major place in his writings, he also belongs with the liberals in his appreciation of Jewish faith as a source of moral and spiritual insight with an integrity of its own.[12] Tillich, incidentally, is quite atypical of German Protestant theology prior to Auschwitz. His thought is wholly uninfected with theological anti-semitism, and, like Barth, he was an early and vigorous Christian opponent of Hitler.

Even in his native Switzerland, Barth has not been the only important prophetic voice. Another Swiss Protestant theologian, Leonhard Ragaz, whose ideas are worth attention, but who has been greatly overshadowed by Barth, belongs at least half-way in the liberal camp. In his brief book on the subject, *Israel, Judaism and Christianity* (English translation), Ragaz accuses Christian piety, especially Lutheranism, of having lapsed into an individualistic concept of redemption which only Judaism, with its rich sense of the earthly presence of God's kingdom, can remedy. (Here he also finds a theological foundation for Chris-

11. See, for example, the debate between David W. Hay and Ellen Flesseman-Van Leer in the *Canadian Journal of Theology:*
Ellen Flesseman-Van Leer, "The Significance of the Mystery of Israel for the Church" (Vol. III/no. 1/January 1957), pps. 5–14; David W. Hay, "The Mystery of Israel: a reply to E. Flesseman-Van Leer" (Vol. III/no. 2/April 1957), pps. 97–101; Ellen Flesseman-Van Leer, "Jew and Gentile: Some Considerations Suggested by Dr. Hay's Reply" (Vol. III/no. 4/October 1957), pps. 235–240.
12. See Bernard Martin, "Paul Tillich and Judaism," *Judaism* (Vol. 15/no. 2/Spring 1966), pps. 180–188.

tian socialism, which was his deepest personal concern.) Like other Christians of a liberal cast, Ragaz desires a mutual exchange of religious insights and values between Judaism and Christianity, benefiting both communities. Unlike most liberals, however, his mind reveals itself as attached to the kerygmatic mode of thinking; he therefore bases his doctrine directly on Romans 9–11. Characteristically Pauline themes are interwoven with characteristically liberal themes: "Thus we are dealing with a twofold fact. Christianity and Judaism belong to Israel. Israel is alive but imperfect, in both. Israel is not embodied in either, nor in both. It flows ceaselessly through them, over them, and in their subterranean depths. And Israel is a judge of both."[13]

In this powerful passage, Ragaz summarizes his own version of the dominant idea underlying all liberal Christian doctrines pertaining to Judaism: an idea which, in one form or another, emerges in the reflections of each of the theologians to be studied in the following pages. Christianity and Judaism, in spite of their historic antagonism and theological differences, possess a common revelatory base in the same sacred scriptures, because they worship the same revealed God of biblical monotheism. This God is always a God of history, associated with the people of the covenant whom Ragaz defines as a kind of mysterious and perfect "Israel" forever greater than any concrete manifestation of Israel in church or synagogue. Christians and Jews, in his theological vision, are therefore custodians of an essentially identical revelation, but each witnesses to this revelation in a variant and imperfect manner. Neither can do without the other (although they are tempted to think so), and neither should try to subsume the other under their own self-identity.

There is a slightly mystical strain in Ragaz. A second and decidedly less mystical example of a liberal Christian doctrine of Judaism is found in the theological writings of the Anglican scholar James Parkes. In contrast to Ragaz, Parkes does not seek

13. Leonhard Ragaz, *Israel, Judaism and Christianity,* London, 1947, p. 63.

the key to Jewish-Christian relations in the theology of Romans 9–11; kerygmatic interpretations of this, or any other section of the New Testament, are highly distasteful to him. Judaism, he believes, is organically linked to Christianity, but ". . . the tension is not some Barthian metaphysic imposed upon history from the outside."[14] Parkes is a liberal of purer breed than Ragaz. All the treasured assumptions of neo-orthodox Protestantism centered around the theological idea of salvation-history are anathema, as far as he is concerned. To him, as to many English churchmen, the anti-rational bias of much continental theology is instinctively uncongenial. His liberalism is of the Pelagian variety.

As a rationalist, therefore, Parkes' approach to the problem begins with man rather than God. The "Barthian metaphysic" to which he objects divides Christians and Jews into two dialectically related communities reflecting the "yes" and "no" of divine mercy and judgment. Instead, as Parkes sees the matter, Christianity and Judaism represent the twin foci of a single overarching revelation addressed to man in the individual and social dimensions of his life. Because these two dimensions of human existence are in a state of "perennial and inevitable" tension,[15] a religion concerned primarily with man as an individual, such as Christianity, lacks a necessary completeness. The other pole of revelation, addressed to man as a social being, is required to compensate for what is absent in Christian religious experience. That, according to Parkes, is the meaning and role of Judaism. Christianity and Judaism therefore belong together in the same structure of faith. They stand "in creative tension with each other,"[16] and must, as a consequence, be accorded equal status and recognition.

Having taken anthropology as his starting point, Parkes de-

14. James Parkes, *The Foundations of Judaism and Christianity*, London, p. 131.
15. *Ibid.*
16. *Ibid.*

velops his doctrine in the same terms. Revelation, he asserts, has enjoyed two great moments in time. At Mount Sinai, God revealed to Moses the true meaning of human community in the Torah. Historically, Judaism is the older religion, for man of necessity had to grasp the secret of his social identity before becoming conscious of his individual identity. Revelation, however, could not cease at that point, for the dawn of a sense of individuality was an inevitable part of the historical process. At Calvary, in keeping with humanity's drive toward individuality, God further revealed "Himself as Person in terms of a human life."[17] The obvious result was Christianity. In the Torah and the Incarnation, the two polar dimensions of man's being are matched with appropriate modes of revelation. But Parkes, interestingly enough, does not cut off the revelatory movement at this historic juncture, although for the sake of consistency he should have done so. Revelation is continuous; hence, somewhat arbitrarily, he is forced to posit a third, rather vague moment of divine self-disclosure in the emergence of modern scientific humanism during the sixteenth and seventeenth centuries of European history.[18] Anthropologically speaking, this corresponds to the intellectual curiosity and creativity of renaissance (and post-renaissance) man, the "seeker after truth."[19] No specific religion, only a quasi-religious secularism, has coalesced around this moment of revelation, but the result nonetheless is a peculiar approximation of the Christian doctrine of the Trinity. In spite of his distrust of classical theology, Parkes, ironically and perhaps unintentionally, concludes with "Father, Son and Holy Spirit," subsuming Judaism under the first category!

Is this type of theology a significant advance over more tradi-

17. Parkes, *God at Work, In Science, Politics and Human Life*, London, 1952, p. 51.
18. *Ibid.*, p. 58.
19. Eckardt, *op. cit.*, p. 83.

tional schemes of salvation history, or a better way of elevating Judaism from its customary low estate in Christian eyes? To a certain measure, Parkes has been successful in this goal, but his doctrine is not without serious theological flaws. What he fails to notice is the manner in which both Judaism and Christianity are actually stripped of their historic uniqueness as religions whose content is immeasurably deeper than other forms of truth. The forward thrust of revelation, the ongoing Spirit, presumably can shape at any time new religious communities whose revelatory inspiration belongs on the same plane as Sinai and Calvary. Inescapably, Judaism becomes less than he desires, as does Christianity also. That which Parkes really seems to be celebrating, in his peculiar trinitarianism, is not Jewish or Christian religious faith, but human progress.

His doctrine, moreover, suffers also from artificiality, although in a less objectionable form than appears in Barth's view of Judaism. It is surely as false to assert that Christianity lacks a true social dimension as it is to assert that Judaism lacks an individual one. The former statement is only valid if one imagines a Christian church utterly divorced from the Old Testament, which, historically, apart from mavericks such as Marcion, has never been the case. Some Christian traditions, Calvinism for example, have been deeply imbued with a sense of social and corporate awareness, occasionally to the point of envisioning the Kingdom of God in almost theocratic terms. Parkes commits basically the same error as Leo Baeck, who, in a famous essay, once described normative Christianity as "romantic" in character,[20] and therefore individualistic in its accent on personal salvation. Judaism, on the other hand, Baeck regarded as the quintessence of "classical" religion, having an immensely deeper ethical dimension. Whether or not he is right about Judaism, he is certainly wrong about forms of Christianity no

20. Leo Baeck, "Romantic Religion," *Judaism and Christianity,* trans. by Walter Kaufmann, New York, 1958, pps. 189–292.

less normative than the pietistic varieties which fit his typology.

In personal terms, Parkes has been a dedicated and courageous foe of anti-semitism all of his career—before, as well as after Auschwitz—and, in some respects, close to a lonely crusader in the Christian world. More than most of his peers, he has made the eradication of anti-semitism a personal *raison d'être*. We have already referred to his important historical investigations in this area.[21] Moreover, unlike all but a still small fraternity of Christians who have taken the trouble to study Judaism seriously, he knows something of its real character and post-Christian evolution. He knows, for example, that Judaism is a living and not a dead religion: a simple fact, but one which eludes many of his fellow-Christians. To appreciate Parkes, one need only compare his views with the following theological judgment of another prominent Anglican, Stephen Neill: "It is within the sphere of the Christian Church, the new Israel, that progress in the knowledge of God has been made, and that revelation has been continuous."[22] In light of this utterance, it is not surprising that Jews, above all, wish a recognition from Christians of the religious vitality and integrity of their faith in the present as well as the past. Judaism is not a fossil; any open-minded person who tests its spirit is quickly driven to the admission that God continues to reveal his presence in the synagogue as well as the church. Neill could not be more wrong.

Such *ex cathedra* pronouncements render a great disservice to Christianity. Because Parkes has devoted his energies to refuting persons such as Neill, he has personified an original prophetic witness that the church can reject only at its peril. That is his greatest contribution. The defects in his theological ventures: his rationalistic bias, his myopia toward aspects of Judaism and Christianity which do not fit into his system, his unconscious

21. Chapter III.
22. Stephen Neill, Introduction, *The Church and the Jewish People,* edited by Goete Hedenquist, London, 1954, pps. 14–15.

depreciation of the two religions, are easily forgivable. Christians, as well as Jews (who have already demonstrated their gratitude), owe this Anglican theologian more recognition than he has received.

Like Ragaz, Parkes exemplifies the fundamental assumption underlying all liberal theologies in which Judaism and Christianity are linked together: despite their differences, the two faiths really constitute the same religion because they are rooted in a common revelation. Remarkably enough, the progenitor of this "Christian" idea was a Jewish intellectual, Franz Rosenzweig, from whose writings not only Ragaz and Parkes, but Niebuhr, Tillich, Eckardt and possibly others, have apparently derived many insights. Because of his strange importance to the church, Rosenzweig is the real center of this chapter.

While corresponding with a Christian friend, Eugen Rosenstock-Huessy,[23] during the years of the First World War, Rosenzweig struggled profoundly with the problems of religious truth. Trembling at one time on the edge of conversion to Christianity, he suddenly drew back in order to reaffirm his Jewish identity in a radical fashion. In his letters of this period one finds his developing ideas concerning the relationship between the church and the synagogue. One excerpt is famous: "Christianity acknowledges the God of the Jews, not as God but as 'the Father of Jesus Christ.' Christianity itself cleaves to the 'Lord' for all time, until the end of the world, but then he will cease to be the Lord, and he too will be subject to the Father who will, on this day, be all in all. . . . No one can reach the Father! But the situation is quite different for one who does

23. "Unlike the mediaeval disputations in which dogma was arrayed against dogma and verse set against verse, this discussion [between Rosenstock-Huessy and Rosenzweig] is a true dialogue. It is indeed the most perfect example of a human approach to the Jewish-Christian problem."
See Alexander Altmann, "Franz Rosenzweig and Eugen Rosenstock-Huessy: An Introduction to their 'Letters on Judaism and Christianity'," *The Journal of Religion* (Vol. XXIV/1944), pps. 258–270.

not have to reach the Father because he is already with him.
And this is true of the people of Israel (though not of individual
Jews). Chosen by the Father, the people of Israel gazes fixedly
across the world and history, over to that last, most distant time
when the Father, the One and Only, will be 'all in all.' Then,
when Christ ceases to be the Lord, Israel will cease to be the
chosen people. . . . But until that day dawns, the lifework of
Israel is to anticipate the eternal day, in profession and in action,
to be its living presage, to hallow the name of God through
its, Israel's, own holiness and with its Law as a people of
priests."[24]

The duty of Judaism is to preserve its life and faith intact;
the duty of Christianity is to evangelize the pagan nations in
the name of the Father already worshipped by the Jews. "The
synagogue knows that what the works of its ritual do for Israel,
the works of love do for the world outside of Israel."[25] Thus,
the inner bond between Christians and Jews is complementary
on the most profound level; their only true difference is one of
function.

According to Hans Joachim Schoeps, Rosenzweig's recognition of the Christian faith as divine in its origins "represents
something basically novel for Judaism . . . it is of extreme
fundamental importance."[26] In a Jewish context, in other words,
Rosenzweig was both an innovator and a great liberal. In a
Christian context, his influence on certain Christian thinkers, although limited largely to this one subject, has not been sufficiently noticed. It is tempting to claim him, like Martin Buber,
as in some sense a crypto-Christian philosopher—thus, for ex-

24. From a letter written to Rudolf Ehrenberg, cited in Nahum N.
Glatzer, *Franz Rosenzweig, His Life and Thought*, New York, 1953,
pps. 341–342.
25. *Ibid.*, p. 342.
26. Hans-Joachim Schoeps, *The Jewish-Christian Argument, A
History of Theologies in Conflict*, trans. by David E. Green, New York,
1963, p. 145.

ample, his mark on Niebuhr: "From the Christian standpoint, the Jews seem to be a nation which has tried desperately to be a church throughout the ages. This is involved in the tension of having a potentially universal religion standing on the historic base of a particular nation. It is this situation which persuaded Franz Rosenzweig to define the relation of Christianity and Judaism as two religions with one center, worshipping the same God, but with Christianity serving the purpose of carrying the prophetic message to the Gentile world. The definition will not satisfy Christians for it obscures some of the real differences between the two religions; but it is better than almost all alternative definitions of the relation between Jew and Christian. . . . It is certainly a better definition than those which prompt Christian missionary activity among the Jews. . . . [Missions] are wrong because the two faiths despite differences are sufficiently alike for the Jew to find God more easily in terms of his own religious heritage than by subjecting himself to the hazards of guilt feeling involved in conversion to a faith, which, whatever its excellencies, must appear to him as a symbol of an oppressive majority culture."[27]

The Jew, for Niebuhr, need not seek God via Christianity. Judaism in its several religious expressions is sufficiently viable as a biblical faith for this purpose: a fact which makes it approximately equal to Christianity, in spite of its ambiguous character as part-nation and part-church. It would be too much to call Niebuhr an unqualified disciple of Rosenzweig, but the latter's influence is clear. Perhaps Niebuhr's confession, in his latest book, of a "long love affair with the Jewish people,"[28] owes a little to the greatness of this Jewish writer.

Tillich also has drawn ideas from Rosenzweig. To Rosen-

27. Reinhold Niebuhr, "The Relations of Christians and Jews in Western Civilization," op. cit., pps. 107–108.
28. Niebuhr, Man's Nature and His Communities, New York, 1965, p. 19.

zweig, the church and the synagogue do not merely coexist in a complementary fashion; they actively and continually need each other. Judaism needs Christianity in order to bring God to the nations, and Christianity needs Judaism in order to protect its own "Jewish" soul. "But the eyes of the synagogue were covered by a band; she saw no world—so how could she have seen gods in it? She could see only by dint of her prophetic inner eye, and she saw nothing but the ultimate, the most remote. . . . That is why, whenever the church forgets she is a stumbling block and desires to become reconciled with what is 'common to all men' . . . the synagogue confronts the church as a silent warner who is not seduced by what is common to all men and knows only of the stumbling block."[29]

The essence of this Rosenzweigian passage is virtually duplicated in one of Tillich's essays: ". . . the Church is always in danger of identifying herself with a national Church, or of leaving injustice, the will-to-power, national and racial arrogance unchallenged. The Church is always in danger of losing its prophetic spirit. Therefore, the prophetic spirit included in the traditions of the Synagogue is needed as long as the gods of time are in power, and this means up to the end of history. . . . Synagogue and Church should be united in our age, in the struggle for the God of time against the gods of space."[30]

Rosenzweig's influence continues to live in modern Protestant theology. His most recent posthumous disciple seems to be the younger American theologian, A. Roy Eckardt, whose recent book, *Elder and Younger Brothers,* is a Christian version of Rosenzweig's doctrine. Eckardt concludes with a decided affirmation of his Jewish mentor's credo: "A Christian theology of the Jewish-Christian relationship is called to proclaim from the Christian side what Franz Rosenzweig has expressed from the Jewish side: Judaism is the 'star of redemption', Christianity

29. Rosenzweig, *op. cit.,* pps. 343–344.
30. Paul Tillich, "The Struggle Between Time and Space," *op. cit.,* p. 39.

the rays of the star. . . . In carrying forward Israel's sacred role, the church does not annul the role of original Israel, nor can it ever, in human history, take the place of Israel. Original Israel continues as the people who 'stay with God', whose enduring task is to sanctify the name of the Lord, to adore the God beyond all the hollow gods of men, to rejoice in and obey the precepts of Torah, to await the coming of God's messianic Kingdom."[31]

Such, in brief, is the mood and spirit of a liberal Protestant doctrine of Judaism.

Without exception, the individual theologians in this chapter have been acutely sensitive to anti-semitism as a critical moral problem for the Christian conscience. Auschwitz is a real presence. Even earlier, persons such as Parkes, or the American church historian, Conrad Moehlman,[32] discerned the depths of the Jewish plight and the measure of Christian complicity. After Auschwitz, better known figures (Niebuhr, Tillich) alike in their concern with the ethical dimensions of faith, took up the cause. Characteristically, Protestant liberalism, especially in the United States with its social gospel heritage, has long been preoccupied with problems of justice, and, for this reason, naturally instrumental in the struggle against inhumanity. But, as we have already observed, Auschwitz happened in Europe, and anti-semitism has never been the critical issue in America as, for example, the race issue has become. Hence, unlike the theological upheavals in the European churches, with their neo-orthodox orientation, no real movement has crystallized in American theology as a liberal counterbalance. Evanston, in this sense, was a one-sided encounter. Not suffering from the guilt feelings of European Christians, the impetus for such a movement has been lacking among the uninvolved Christian population of the United States. The liberal impulse toward the

31. Eckardt, *op. cit.,* p. 160.
32. Moehlman is the author of a non-theological work, *The Jewish-Christian Tragedy, A Study in Religious Prejudice,* Rochester, 1933.

Jews, consequently, has been articulated by a few theologians only. These have sounded no uncertain trumpet, but not many have followed!

This is certainly a misfortune. For continental theology in all its forms badly needs a counterbalance. Auschwitz is the haunting memory in the minds of Catholic and Protestant theologians in Europe who have written about the Jews, and to even the most conservative of the foregoing, the crisis this memory poses for the church has been clear. But the obligation felt by such writers, especially the Catholics, to defend the deposit of sacred tradition or traditional exegesis has seriously restricted their contribution to a new understanding. Still worse, the older Catholic attitude toward revealed truth, in this context, has tragically debased the status of the love commandment, which, in greater or lesser degree, must be forcibly reconciled with a body of anti-Jewish "true" dogma. In their own way, Protestant biblicists have been quite as guilty of the same sin, even intensifying it. For less kerygmatic thinkers, on the other hand, no such defensiveness is required. Not only do liberal theologians reject in any case the patristic image of Judaism, but, because liberal Christianity has different priorities, any conflict between the claims of "truth" and the claims of love, such as permeates every conservative theology dealing with the subject, is not a problem. Love is the only valid dogma. The premise here is simple enough. A religion centered around a God whose supreme self-revelation is his nature as a God of love, cannot, on the theological level, endorse doctrines that are obviously hurtful and unloving without betraying its most profound commitment. Although this basic assertion of liberal Christianity can result in a suspicion of even inoffensive doctrines, simply because they were formulated in other ages,[33] the release it affords from apologetic and defensive attitudes is a great gain.

33. Parkes, for example, reveals a curiously anti-Pauline bias when he comments on Romans. See his book, *The Foundations of Judaism and Christianity.*

148

Although the radical (or biblical) theologians in both the Catholic and Protestant worlds are neither defensive nor, in a bad sense, apologetic, they too cling to a kerygmatic approach, believing, with total Christian one-sidedness, that Jew and Christian must understand each other according to the New Testament, especially as their relationship is defined in Romans 9–11. The rigidity of this view has already been protested. While Paul's great chapters are incomparable in their general profundity and spiritual insight, and while it is important for modern Christians to recapture the apostle's sense of personal kinship with "original Israel" (Eckardt), to whom belongs "the sonship, the glory, the covenants, the giving of the law, the worship, and the promises. . . . ,'[34] if Romans 9–11 are literalized, distortions are inevitable. Transformed into a kerygma, Paul's words will hinder, not help, a Jewish-Christian *rapprochement,* although their "illustrative" value (Sittler) is a different matter entirely. Thus, the radical theologians also must be corrected by a still more radical standard: that of love.

Before the danger of dogmatic one-sidedness, the characteristic openness of liberal theology to the the divine presence in non-Christian religions provides a potential safeguard. Ragaz, Parkes, Niebuhr, Tillich and Eckardt all demonstrate a capacity to recognize the abiding worth and religious power of Judaism, even if they do not define its most vital qualities in identical terms. This capacity, perhaps, is made easier by the natural sympathy of Christian liberals with the dominant ethical flavor of Jewish faith. No Christian, probably, can succeed entirely in grasping the genius of Judaism from the inner perspective of a Jew (an elusive art in any case, although something that dialogue must nonetheless attempt). Moreover, even the most liberal theologian is controlled by his own viewpoint, and, in a sense, makes use of whatever elements in Judaism best suit his purposes. To Ragaz, Judaism's "earthly" apprehension of God's kingdom is, for a Christian socialist, its deepest value; to Parkes,

34. Romans 9:4.

Judaism's revelation of the social dimensions of religious morality—a somewhat broader concept—is its gift to the world; to Niebuhr, Judaism's "civic virtues" are paramount; to Tillich, the Jewish witness to the "God of time" against human idolatries is Judaism's greatest significance; to Eckardt, Judaism's covenantal fidelity makes the synagogue the perennial "elder brother" of the church, and, in this respect, its spiritual model. If these qualities are not dissimilar, neither are they exactly the same. Some distortions are therefore evident in liberal as well as in conservative theologies pertaining to the subject. But distorted ideas based upon a genuine appreciation and recognition of Judaism are always preferable to distorted ideas based upon Christian presuppositions which grant Judaism no religious rights whatever.

Rosenzweig has been described as the real center of this chapter: almost, in fact, as a visionary mediator between Judaism and Christianity. This should not imply, however, an uncritical acceptance on the author's part of Rosenzweig's thesis that the two religions are really one religion, divided only for reasons of function and historical accident. There is a strain of idealism in this concept that affects the judgment of both Rosenzweig himself and some of his Christian imitators. When Rosenzweig speaks of the purity of Judaism's inner vision of God, he seems to idealize the interior life of the pious ghetto Jew whose place in European society had been severely restricted by historic circumstances. Is Judaism really as immune to idolatry as he thinks? Moreover, are Judaism and Christianity really as complementary as he imagines? A modern Jewish theologian, Jakob Petuchowski, speaks of a lack of realism in such liberals as Rosenzweig and Parkes when they call for mutual recognition between Jews and Christians.[35] While Niebuhr (a genuine realist) is obviously conscious of the limitations of any defini-

35. Jakob J. Petuchowski, "The Christian-Jewish Dialog: A Jewish View," *Lutheran World* (Vol. X/no. 4/October 1963), p. 384.

tion that pretends that no real issue lies between Judaism and Christianity, Parkes does not accept this premise. As we have seen, he slavishly follows Rosenzweig in insisting on a neat and logical division of vocations—minus Rosenzweig's mystical fervor. There is no room in his system for the assertion, made by a neo-orthodox theologian, that Judaism and Christianity exist in a state of mutual tension, and must therefore "question each other until the end of time."[36] But here Jocz shows more realism than Parkes, who clings to the illusion of perfect compatibility and equality of function.

A factor which should not be neglected in evaluating Rosenzweig's mode of relating the two religious communities is the variety within Judaism itself. Instead of Judaism as a single religious system, it is probably more accurate to speak of several Jewish approaches to faith. Reform Judaism, the most liberal religious style among Jews, not only shares many traits with the more liberal versions of Protestant Christianity, but represents that segment of Jewish opinion most likely to see itself (and Christianity) in Rosenzweigian terms. On the other hand, Orthodox Judaism, judging from its present mood, is much less likely to see itself in such a fashion, although the Orthodox stress on revelation accords better with traditional Christian theology. At least one major Jewish theologian, Joseph Soloveitchik, believes that the gulf between Christianity and Judaism is too great for even a meaningful question-and-answer dialogue. On the religious level, in his view, the two faiths are so radically different as to constitute two solitudes, as it were, and cannot communicate in depth at all.[37] Soloveitchik is the antithesis of Rosenzweig.

36. Jakob Jocz, *The Jewish People and Jesus Christ: A Study in the Relationship between the Jewish People and Jesus Christ,* London, 1949, p. 264.

37. There is an excellent summary of Soloveitchik's theology in Eugene B. Borowitz, *A New Jewish Theology in the Making,* Philadelphia, 1968, pp. 160–173.

Rosenzweig, therefore, is subject to criticism. One must ask, in light of this criticism, if the case for a liberal doctrine falls to pieces if Rosenzweig's particular definition of the relationship between the church and the synagogue is rejected. The answer has to be no. Cannot a measure of mutual tension, springing from some basic differences, be acknowledged, without forgetting the family similarities between Christian faith and Jewish faith? Is it not possible to discern God's revelatory presence in a religious community that, in part, contradicts the treasured assumptions and loyalties of one's own religious heritage and religious commitment? Cannot a Christian liberalism retain its broadness of vision without expressing its convictions in idealized theological pictures which distort the real images of life? What the contemporary situation requires is not the repudiation of Rosenzweig, but a realistic revision of his basic insights. It is not necessary to swing in the opposite direction with Soloveitchik in order to bow the knee before reality.

In making these revisions, some guidelines should be kept in mind. *Pace* Rosenzweig, Judaism and Christianity do not fit naturally into a mold which seeks to merge their differences by conceiving them as only differing limbs on the same body. They must be forced into such a mold. (Soloveitchik is right in regarding each religion as an autonomous totality, with individual and social dimensions accordingly; he is wrong only in believing that no communication is possible between their representatives.) It is extremely dubious also as to whether Judaism can be described—as Rosenzweig thought—as a non-missionary form of religious faith preoccupied essentially with its own spiritual purity and self-preservation. Petuchowski, for one, denies the validity of this description. "And does not the Jew, too, live in the expectation of an ultimate conversion of the gentiles to the faith of Israel? The passage from Maimonides (cited early by Petuchowski) . . . goes on to say: 'But when the true Messiah comes, the nations (missionized by Christianity and Islam) will immediately repent and realize that . . . their fathers have caused them to inherit falsehood, and that their prophets have led them astray.' There is no unanimity in Judaism whether the ultimate 'conversion of the gentiles' for which the synagogue daily prays . . . implies conversion to Israel's cult as well as to Israel's God. . . . But there can be no doubt that, theologically speaking, Judaism does expect a redeemed mankind to be strict monotheists—in the *Jewish* sense."[38]

Can any religion seriously committed to religious monotheism avoid, in principle if not in practice, a missionary character? Monotheism, by its very nature, does not allow room for other gods. Judaism, moreover, at one time in its history, actively engaged in proselytism before the Christian state forced the synagogue to withdraw from overt convert-seeking.[39] Nonetheless, a rival universalism, never totally suppressed, remains implicit in Jewish faith and theology today. Thus, as Petuchowski insists, Judaism cannot be reduced to a religion whose only focus is an interior concentration on God. Surely, Martin Buber was more perceptive than Rosenzweig when he recognized a partially concealed tension between Judaism and Christianity arising from the clash of their opposing universalistic claims. His definition is famous: "Pre-messianically our destinies are divided. Now to the Christian the Jew is the incomprehensibly obdurate man, who declines to see what has happened; and to the Jew the Christian is the incomprehensibly daring man, who affirms in an unredeemed world that its redemption has been accomplished."[40]

Still, Rosenzweig's great affirmation of an unique spiritual kinship between the church and the synagogue as brother religious communities, whose existence would be meaningless apart

38. Petuchowski, *op. cit.,* p. 381.
39. Jewish proselytism may have lasted as late as the fifth Christian century. See Flannery, *op. cit.,* p. 39.
40. Martin Buber, "The Two Foci of the Jewish Soul," *Israel and the World,* New York, 1948, p. 40.

from the living God of biblical monotheism, is fully convincing. In this sense, he was right in describing Christians and Jews as sharers of the same revelation. The church, after all, began its career as a Jewish sect, and, as post-Auschwitz Christian theologians of varying types have seen with increasing clarity, a Christianity which discriminates against its Jewishness quickly dries up its own soul. (It is no accident, incidentally, that the most prominent of the contemporary "death-of-God" theologians, Thomas Altizer, seems, in many respects, a modern Marcion, intent on wrenching the Christian gospel completely free from its Jewish matrix.[41]) On that point, Catholics and Protestants, traditionalists and radicals, neo-orthodox and liberal thinkers, agree. Hitler has been a cruel tutor as far as this elementary lesson is concerned. But the man indirectly most responsible for teaching the church in the twentieth century the most important truth about itself is Franz Rosenzweig.

Rosenzweig's Christian followers have been few. Despite their small company, however, they have done more than remind the Christian world of the fact that Christianity is, in essence, a form of Judaism. They have enabled Christians to glimpse the religious grandeur of their hitherto maligned and misunderstood historic neighbors: the Jews. To the present as well as the past, they have opened a window which traditional theology had long since slammed shut.

---

41. I am referring to Altizer's determination to liberate the "Incarnate Word" from every past moment of historical fulfillment in the interest of ever-new, ongoing epiphanies. "To confine theological meaning to the sacred history and scriptures of the past is to abjure the activity of the Word in the present and to reverse the kenotic direction of the uniquely Christian Word." The logic of this statement implies that Christianity should seek new revelations wholly detached from its Judaic heritage.

I am indebted to Dr. Jakob Petuchowski for drawing my attention to Altizer in this context.

See Thomas J. J. Altizer, *The Gospel of Christian Atheism*, Philadelphia, 1966, pps. 82f.

VIII. The Jews in an Ecumenical Context:

A Critique

Everyone knows that the ecumenical movement is concerned with matters of Christian unity. As such, according to William Temple, it represents a great new fact of our century. Theoretically, one would naturally assume, ecumenism has no logical connection with problems of Jewish-Christian relations, except insofar as Christian missionary strategy (one of the early concerns of the movement) might touch upon the Jews. But evidently, the obvious is not really obvious. Robert McAfee Brown, in his study, *The Ecumenical Revolution,* notes that the ecumenical concept has been quietly enlarged in modern times. Now it embraces not only Christians of widely different persuasions, Roman Catholic as well as Protestant and Orthodox, and even some sectarian groups, but Jews as well.[1] In what sense can a movement born out of a desire for Christian reunion properly occupy itself with either Judaism, as a non-Christian religion, or the Jewish people as a historic entity?

Ambiguity, as Brown recognizes, is one immediate result of

1. Robert M. Brown, *The Ecumenical Revolution, An Interpretation of the Catholic-Protestant Dialogue,* New York, 1967, pps. 247–276.

this "new" great new fact of the twentieth century. The word "ecumenical," which hitherto has implied only a Christian frame of reference, must now suggest a certain extra-Christian meaning as well, namely "a spirit of co-operation and good will among all men, whatever their theological or religious presuppositions."[2] On this level, the ambiguity is not serious, but it becomes serious as soon as the radical biblical ideas concerning the Jews described in previous chapters are taken into account. For the "schism" theologians, as we have seen, Jewish-Christian relations are the core of the ecumenical quest, not a secondary matter on its edge. Unless, in their view, the church re-establishes its primordial unity with the other part of the people of God, the Jews, it is destined to incompleteness and failure in its minor ecumenical goals. Ecumenism, consequently, is defined in a fashion which is at almost total variance with its older definition. The confusion which has followed, especially at Evanston, is scarcely surprising. Can this new definition be accepted as a viable theological foundation for the ecumenical movement and its programs?

One of the apparent virtues of the schism doctrine lies in its substitution of a dialogue relationship with Jews in place of the older Christian practice of direct proselytizing. The idea of dialogue is one of the enthusiasms of the ecumenical age, but, curiously enough, this enthusiasm is not unanimous. Barth, for example, is a major dissenter. No throwback to the past, he is deeply adamant in his opposition to Jewish missions in the traditional sense.[3] He is not, however, against converting Jews to Christianity, but sees little merit in conversations, except for exchanging information, since merely talking is unlikely to produce any spiritual fruit. After all, nothing less than the "direc-

2. *Ibid.,* pps. 246–247.
3. Karl Barth, *Church Dogmatics,* Vol. IV/3/2, p. 877, fn. "Mission is not the witness which it [the church] owes to Israel. When Paul sought to be a Jew to Jews, it was not just formally but materially *toto caelo* different from when he sought to be a Greek to the Greeks."

tion intervention of God Himself" sufficed to bring that "most obstinate of all Jews, Paul," to a state of conversion.[4] If the matter is up to God, what is the point of a dialogue? It is better to leave the Jews alone. Barth's solution, therefore, is neither missionary nor dialogical, but eschatological. At some moment in time, presumably, God will intervene again, and that will be that. (Some Jewish critics, incidentally, have not found this attitude too objectionable, for example André Neher.[5] It is also worth noting, in this context, the interesting parallel between Barth and Soloveitchik in their respective attitudes toward inter-religious dialogue. Soloveitchik regards dialogue as a futile enter-prise for at least partly similar reasons to Barth, although from a Jewish standpoint. Not without cause, he has been styled a Jewish "Karl Barth.")

While Barth's imitators and disciples are equally emphatic in their disdain for missions,[6] they, including his son Markus,[7] evince greater enthusiasm for a dialogue encounter, in keeping with the ecumenical spirit. They mean, however, something more than merely extending to Jews the same courtesy and qualified recognition that prevail among the Christian partners in the ecumenical experiment. One does not have to read much of the relevant literature in order to discover that dialogue, in

4. *Ibid.*, pps. 877–878.

5. See Neher's article, "Le Juif face au Chrétien," *Foi et Vie,* 9e Cahier d'Études Juives (no. 6/1959), pps. 3–9.

Neher refers to Démann rather than Barth, but the point is the same.

6. The following "thesis" by Guenter Harder is typical:

"Dagegen respektiert sie [the church] die Entscheidung der Juden-schaft, die Jesus nicht als ihren Messias anerkennt, als besonderen Weg goettlicher Entscheidung und versucht nicht, durch besondere mission-arische Unternehmungen und Einrichtungen herbeizufuehren, was Gott sich fuer seine Zukunft verbehalten hat."

See "Mission und Gespraech—10 Thesen," *Das Gespaltene Gottes-volk,* p. 283. See also *Israel und die Kirche,* pps. 41–44, and other writings.

7. Markus Barth, *The Broken Wall: A Study of the Epistle to the Ephesians,* Chicago, 1959, pps. 133–134.

relation to Judaism, has a special character. The schism theologians are in favor of a Jewish-Christian dialogue for the same reason that Barth is against this form of encounter: they wish to promote the conversion of Jews to Christianity. That is its *raison d'être*. Talking, they believe, will produce spiritual fruit, provided that the Christian participants take seriously their responsibility to witness in the presence of their Jewish counterparts to the truth of their faith. Whatever such a dialogue means, it "does not mean any religious levelling or renunciation of the special Christian witness, which must be given even in the context of dialogue, where it is always necessary."[8]

In a long essay published in *Der ungekuendigte Bund,* Guenter Harder elaborates his statement. "From there, that double Christian relation to the synagogue is understood as a 'yes' to the latter, insofar as it is the elect people of God, united in itself and religiously relevant in its manifestation, but a 'no' insofar as this unity occurs outside of the name of Jesus . . ."[9] Later, in the same essay, he adds: "Christianity ought not simply to repeat each sentence in the biting style of John's Gospel, thinking that thereby its witness is sufficient, but Christianity is called to witness to Christ, its contemporary living Lord, in the context of its now mature dialogue with Judaism, as the messiah of the people of God formed of both Jews and Gentiles."[10]

This theological circumscription of the dialogue encounter is extremely revealing. Missions, in the traditional sense, are passé, but Jews must still expect to be told, sooner or later, that their Judaism is misguided, and that they can only find religious authenticity, as the elect people, by bringing their gifts to the church. Here again, Romans 9–11 is an obvious intruder. This is

8. Guenter Harder, *op. cit.,* p. 283. My translation.
9. Harder, "Das Christlich-Juedische Gespraech im Verhaeltnis zum Christlichen Zeugnis an Israel," *Der ungekuendigte Bund,* p. 146. My translation.
10. *Ibid.,* p. 156. My translation.

exactly what Paul envisaged.[11] To read some theologians (Torrance, for example),[12] one gathers that Jews almost owe the church the moral duty of becoming Christians, so that the spiritually enervated Gentiles can receive the transfusion of faith which the mass conversion of the Jewish community alone can guarantee!

It does not require enormous discernment to see that this kind of ecumenism verges on the bogus. Missions in the old mold may be disavowed, but the logic of a dialogue that is premised on the superiority of Christian categories cannot avoid a conversionist *telos,* however obligue or muted. Jews, as might be expected, are not slow to decipher the hidden assumptions. Thus, Steven Schwarzschild reacts strongly against such efforts to lure Judaism inside the ecumenical enterprise: "Neither Ecumenism, which is an exclusively Christian endeavour, nor Scriptures, about the nature of which we substantially disagree, can bind together Christian and Jews."[13] Schwarzschild's response may seem unduly cold, but Christians are foolish if they believe that an "ecumenical" approach to the Jews can possibly succeed when, in effect, it amounts to little more than an invitation to join the church. Such a use of dialogue is basically ideological in nature, and only a minor improvement over direct missionary strategies. To some, it might seem less honest.

Unfortunately, the promotion of dialogue in the hope of securing religious conversions is becoming popular in certain Christian circles today. Another example is George A. F. Knight, who, in a book designed to equip Christians for an apologetic struggle with Jews, says much the same as Harder: ". . . the Christian cannot rest content even with dialogue, even when it is carried on in complete humility and love. . . . Ultimately . . .

11. Romans 11:12.
12. Torrance, *op. cit.*
13. Steven S. Schwarzschild, "Judaism, Scriptures and Ecumenism," *Judaism* (Vol. 13/no. 3/1964), p. 268.

the Christian must go beyond the area of dialogue, for he must ceaselessly witness to the Christ who is greater than his own faith and greater than his own understanding of what Christianity may be."[14]

The exposé is complete. Christians, in Knight's view, must go *beyond* dialogue; in other words, Knight is not really interested in dialogue at all! He is interested in conversion. In company with Harder, he labors under the misconception that not to be interested in conversion involves some form of disloyalty to Christ, and a betrayal of the Christian faith. But "witness" may have a different meaning entirely from the imperialistic meaning which arises from this conventional interpretation. Knight, furthermore, exposes his true understanding of dialogue when he reveals the low esteem in which he holds modern Judaism. A "schism" theologian (although an Anglo-Saxon scholar), he succeeds, like Barth, in stating this doctrine in terms which imply a highly denigratory opinion of the spiritual condition of the Jewish soul. "Israel, then, is one indeed, but the mystery of Israel is this, that it is one in the sense that Siamese twins are one. Only, in this case, one of the twins . . . has accepted in humility and boundless gratitude all that God, in his grace, has done to include him in the completion, the perfection, the wholeness, the *pleroma* of all things. The other twin has not, for he believes that, as Israel, unlike the Gentiles, he is already living in the presence of God."[15]

But a dialogue between someone who knows that he possesses the *pleroma* of all things, and someone who does not, is not a dialogue at all; it is a monologue in which questions of truth are already foreclosed, so that the Jew must listen while the Christian speaks. Dialogues of this type were common in the Middle Ages, and, as far as the church is concerned, they

14. George A. F. Knight, "Beyond Dialogue," *Jews and Christians: Preparation for Dialogue,* Philadelphia, 1965, pps. 176–177.
15. Knight, "The Mystery of Israel," *ibid.,* p. 56.

represent an episode in Christian history that is better forgotten. No matter how painstakingly the schism theologians who wish to witness to the Jews in the context of dialogue seek to sound a more circumspect note than the false dialogues of the past, the fact remains that their "ecumenical" approach is tainted with a measure of the same Christian imperialism. This, for the most part, is undoubtedly unintentional, but it is true nonetheless. Properly seen, what appears initially as a virtue in post-Auschwitz Catholic and Protestant theology is, at best, only a modified vice. Proselytism in a new guise has appeared on the scene.

As spokesman for a fresh style of ecumenism, therefore, these theologians are unwise counsellors. An ecumenical movement whose foundations rest on an infallible kerygmatic interpretation of Romans 9–11 has little chance of achieving its goals, for hidden in its credo is the same image of the unbelieving Jew which the church has projected on Jewish history for centuries. Christians, however, have paid a heavy price for regarding Judaism in this fashion. They have created for themselves a tragic psychological "predicament" (Bokser) that has harmed the church spiritually almost as much as it has harmed Jews physically. "The endeavour of Christianity to appropriate Judaism as a stage in its own development is challenged by the abiding loyalty of Jews to Judaism, while the eagerness of Christianity to convert Jews derives from the necessity to substantiate the basic claim of Christian doctrine. The resistance of Jews to the missionary activities of the Church thus becomes a basic Christian frustration, an affront and a threat to the Christian image of itself. Those who are frustrated are always tempted to translate their frustration into hostility toward those responsible for their predicament."[16]

Any Christian who, in dialogue, is anxious to convert his Jewish counterpart only succeeds in exposing a persistent sickness in

16. Bokser, *op. cit.,* pps. 34–35.

Christian piety that continues to plague Jewish-Christian relations. The identical compulsion, described by Bokser, which lies behind every proselytizing campaign aimed at the Jews from medieval times until today, is capable of operating even when Christians think themselves tolerant and sophisticated, as long as its root theological cause survives. Must not the synagogue be rescued from its inexplicable disbelief (Romans 9–11)? New-breed theologians such as Harder, Knight and Torrance seem to exemplify this anxiety perfectly. Without knowing it, they destroy dialogue at its moment of birth. They fail to understand that most Jews would prefer the cessation of all relationships with Christians, even at the cost of social ostracism and personal danger, rather than accept a relationship in which they are basically regarded as objects for conversion. When Abraham Heschel insists that "unless the church will give up the 'mission to the Jews' there can be no dialogue,"[17] he intends, I suspect, more than a repudiation of old-style proselytism. Almost certainly, his criticism extends to the semi-disguised conversionist ideology of ecumenical Christians, who through dialogue have seized a new means of communicating the gospel to the descendants of the original generation of "stubborn disbelievers," whose refusal to accept Christ provided the church with its first great thorn in the flesh. The compulsion still throbs.

An ecumenism dominated by such a mindset offers no hope. This should not mean, however, that an ecumenical relationship between Jews and Christians cannot be achieved in other terms, nor, in spite of Schwarzschild, that the word "ecumenical" is a misnomer in this context. With Rosenzweig, it is possible to maintain that Christianity and Judaism bear a peculiar kinship to each other infinitely deeper than any tie that either bears to any other religious community. Naturally, if one defines ecumen-

17. Abraham J. Heschel, "From Mission to Dialogue," *Conservative Judaism* (Vol. XXI/no. 3/Spring 1967), p. 11.

ism as a generalized "spirit of co-operation and good will among all men, whatever their theological or religious presuppositions," an ecumenical relationship is possible between Christians and Hindus, Christians and Muslims, or Christians and Marxists. But a special dimension is involved in the relationship between Jews and Christians, who share the same unique God of biblical monotheism: a God whose essential features are less clearly delineated in that other monotheistic faith, Islam. If the theologians who stand in the Rosenzweigian stream—the liberals of the previous chapter—are right in their basic assumption concerning Judaism and Christianity, a genuine dialogue, that is, a dialogue that is not on the Christian side merely an ideological plea for conversion, should not only be possible, but instinctive and natural between Jews and Christians. Individuals who employ the same language of faith, because they share the same Hebrew scriptures, ought to communicate more easily than the representatives of much less similar religious communities (although dialogue is by no means impossible in the latter case). The spiritual children of Abraham stand apart.

In placing the Jewish-Christian encounter in a more adequate setting than the narrow confines of Romans 9–11, with their Christian one-sidedness, can allow, a further comment should be made on the subject of conversion. To deny that consciously seeking to convert one's non-Christian partner is a legitimate goal in a religious dialogue does not imply a denial of the reality or validity of conversion itself. Obviously, conversions do occur, and the possibility of conversion is always present in every existential meeting as a risk which the participants must accept. But it is a risk on both sides. The Christian may become a Jew, as well as the Jew a Christian. Or, alternatively, the Christian may reaffirm his Christianity in a more profound way, and the Jew his Judaism in a more profound way (thus Rosenzweig). If one is unwilling to accept the risk of conversion, one should not engage in this kind of dialogue in the first place, for

163

a true personal encounter requires the investment of a man's entire religious being. Except in this sense, the possibility of conversion is not a barrier to dialogue, but part of the process of any "I-Thou" meeting. Not even the prior knowledge that either or both religions involved are missionary faiths with universalistic claims is a barrier,[18] unless this knowledge is permitted to turn the encounter into a contest that can only end with victor and vanquished. Rather, what is fatal is the *idée fixé* that subverts every conversation in order to achieve a predetermined goal of conversion, and judges it worthless otherwise. To do this, one must assume (as all absolutists do) that a monopoly of truth or revelation—the *pleroma* of all things—lies on one's own side, that is, the church, and that the other side is spiritually bankrupt.

But dialogue on these terms is certain to prove stillborn. An authentic dialogue is only possible if revelation is in some sense shared, or, as Tillich declares, if "both partners acknowledge the value of the other's religious conviction (as based ultimately on a revelatory experience). . . ."[19] Needless to say, this is not an easy concession. No one lightly undergoes the agony of permitting old and sanctified preconceptions to die, especially a church long accustomed to encasing its faith in an absolutistic theology, and no one readily approaches a stranger truly expecting to discover God in unfamiliar places. Yet this is the quality

18. According to J. R. Chandran, Christians and Hindus have had successful dialogues in India despite the knowledge on the part of the Hindu representatives that Christianity was a missionary faith. I assume, of course, that these dialogues were free from any form of manipulation designed to convert the Hindus directly. It should also be remembered that no history of bad feelings exists between Hindus and Christians as a counterpart of the long religious conflict between Jews and Christians.

See J. R. Chandran, "Discussion: Christianity and Other Faiths," *Union Seminary Quarterly Review* (January, 1965/Vol. XX/no. 2), p. 183.

19. Paul Tillich, *Christianity and the Encounter of the World Religions*, New York, 1963, p. 62.

THE JEWS IN AN ECUMENICAL CONTEXT

of spirit that religious dialogue demands, and which Christians and Jews must both be willing to attain. Otherwise, they should settle, as Soloveitchik suggests, for a different *modus vivendi* of religious co-existence.

Theoretically, as the spiritual heirs of the Abrahamic legacy, Christians and Jews ought to provide a model of everything that religious dialogue should mean. Practically, this is much less certain. Anti-semitism has poisoned their relationship for too protracted a period. Many Jews remain seriously suspicious of Christian intentions in a dialogue-encounter, and sceptical of its advantages. Berkovits, Soloveitchik and Schwarzschild are examples. To the latter, the age immediately after Auschwitz is suitable for silence, not conversation. "But between Jews and Christians this is perhaps the time for silence, as it was the time to speak out twenty-five years ago. After the storm is over—if it is over—nature, like the spirit, needs a long moment to catch its breath, to put things into proper perspective, to gather its wits, to contemplate the reality of the situation, to assess the damage that was done, to consider the individual's position in the new scheme of things. A generation from now the pieces may fall into place . . . Right now, our Egypt is barely behind us, and the Promised Land is still far away. We are the generation of the desert, no longer willing to live under the slave-master, not yet ready for freedom, certainly incapable of easy fraternization between master and liberated slave."[20]

This melancholy conclusion is supported by the manner in which Christian religious symbols have suffered corruption in Jewish eyes because of the use to which the church has put them. The cross, supremely identified by Christians with the love and mercy of God, scarcely evokes the same emotional response in Jews who have been burned by the fires of Auschwitz, and suspect that historic Christendom helped to light the blaze. Even Christian piety is suspected, for faith is interwoven with theol-

20. Schwarzschild, *op., cit.,* p. 265.

ogy, and doctrines are meant to be believed. Given the anti-Jewish character of so much of Christian tradition, one can appreciate an observation which I once heard Reinhold Niebuhr make in a classroom, that "the more pious Christians are, the more anti-semitic Jews assume they will be."[21] This comment does not lose its relevance when Christians are devoid of piety, for the possibility of a change of heart is always present.

To judge by the sporadic and half-successful attempts at a Jewish-Christian dialogue in the nineteen-sixties, Schwarzschild's reflections match the historical situation with reasonable accuracy. Christian-Jewish relations are still quite fragile, and, as the "silence of the churches"[22] during the Arab-Israeli War, June, 1967, demonstrates, they are easily shattered. Some individual dialogues, to be sure, have been fruitful,[23] but, on the whole, it cannot be said that a spirit of reconciliation has swept the majority of churches and synagogues. On the Jewish side, the large and important Orthodox community continues to hold itself aloof. On the Christian side, the struggle for a revised estimate of Judaism is still contending with the heavy weight of theological prejudice, as well as secular anti-semitism. Interestingly enough, in America at least, Catholics are currently showing a greater willingness to engage in the dialogue venture than Protestants. Nevertheless, if an ecumenical relationship is spoken of at all between Judaism and Christianity, the present state of affairs requires that the term "ecumenical" be used in a nascent rather than a developed sense.

Assuming, however, that Jews and Christians, in spite of everything, do muster the will to meet on a more than super-

21. At Union Seminary, New York, 1960.
22. Eckardt, "Again, Silence in the Churches," *Elder and Younger Brothers,* pps. 163–177.
23. For example, Philip Scharper (editor), *Torah and Gospel, Jewish and Catholic Theology in Dialogue,* New York, 1966; Katherine T. Hargrove (editor), *The Star and the Cross, Essays on Jewish-Christian Relations,* Milwaukee, 1966; and others.

ficial basis, they must immediately face a double task. Any dialogue can serve two purposes. One purpose is the elimination of mutual misconceptions—what Arthur Gilbert has called the "exorcism of demons"[24]—in order that each religious partner might grasp the real rather than imagined character of the other's worldview. Obviously, a great deal of exorcising must take precedence over any other form of discussion in which the representatives of Judaism and Christianity are involved. The demons are numerous indeed. But once this preliminary purpose of dialogue has been completed, the encounter acquires a deeper dimension. Jew and Christian can then face each other robed in the true garments of their respective faiths, each recognizing the other with a measure of authenticity. The purpose of dialogue then becomes a mutual search, in terms of both traditions, for new light and clarity concerning the human situation.

Such dialogues (in the deeper sense) can and have taken place among select individuals. The remarkable dialogue between Rosenzweig and Rosenstock-Huessy, to which we have already referred, is probably the best known modern example. When a dialogue reaches this point of genuine maturity, it necessarily concentrates on the most fundamental religious questions. One such question which must figure in any in-depth conversation between Jews and Christians has been succinctly stated by Buber: is the world, as the church claims, already redeemed, or is it still, as Judaism claims, in an unredeemed condition? Of course, this definition of the tension between Judaism and Christianity is not the only matter at stake; if the whole difference between the two religions were reducible to Buber's formula, one might describe their theological and historical apposition as the consequence of nothing more than a quarrel about time.[25]

24. See Arthur Gilbert's response to my article, "The Jews in an Ecumenical Context: A Critique," *Journal of Ecumenical Studies* (Vol. V/Summer 1968/no. 3), p. 576.

25. It should not be overlooked, of course, that Christianity also has a futurist dimension, and regards redemption as in some sense still to

Yet this issue is one critical aspect of the encounter of the two religious worldviews upon which a serious dialogue must inevitably focus, after the demons have been purged and a basic rapport achieved. Tillich locates another fundamental question in the conflicting attitudes of Judaism and Christianity toward the problem of religious guilt.[26]

Although a few Jews and Christians have succeeded in crossing the threshold of dialogue in its fullest possibilities, the majority, if Schwarzschild is correct, are not yet able to sustain an ecumenical meeting on such a sensitive and intimate level. Too many unhealed wounds continue to fester. For the moment, therefore, the first purpose of dialogue, getting rid of the demons, is probably the only realistic goal. The *kairos* is surely right for a beginning.

Let us turn, then, to the demons. The church is already in the throes of exorcising the demons of deicide, malediction, degeneracy, from its theological tradition. Of the demons which remain, probably the most subtle is lodged, as we have seen, in the Pauline image of the Jew as a special species of non-believer, somehow more culpable than the other opponents of Christianity among the religious and anti-religious communities of mankind. Romans 9–11 is inadvertently responsible for this image, but, as we have stressed, spiritual blindness can never be an adequate conceptualization of the inner mind and heart of Judaism. Admittedly, the larger portion of ancient Israel said "no" to the gospel, but even Paul, who wrestled deeply with this response, did not suggest that the Judaism of his age had

---

come. The recent theologies of "hope" (for example, Moltmann) are closer to Judaism in this respect than old theological concepts of time. But it seems to me that Rosemary Ruether dissolves Christianity into Judaism when she apparently denies any past historical fulfillment of a once-and-for-all character as far as the christological faith of the church is concerned.

See Ruether, *op. cit.*

26. See D. Mackenzie Brown, *Ultimate Concern, Tillich in Dialogue,* New York, 1965, pp. 113–115.

irreligious motivations in its decision against Christianity. Rather, in his opinion, the Jews possessed an over-abundance of religious zeal.[27] As Stendahl writes, "To Paul, the Jew, this 'no' [of the Jews to Jesus] was a mystery which he treated with awe, and which, according to him, should create greater awe and reverence in Gentile minds (Rom. 11:20)."[28]

Unfortunately, later Christian theologians, not being participants—as Paul was—in a highly personal struggle during a time when "the unfolding meaning of God's work in the midst of his People was still a dynamic open question,"[29] did not grasp his point. Perhaps they lacked the necessary degree of historical imagination as well as the necessary degree of religious tolerance. In any case, the theological results of their failure are now commonplace. Judaism, as we have seen, became transformed into a religion without right or favor, a "theological device, a *ficelle* of Christian history,"[30] instead of a living and legitimate faith.

For this reason, a demon of sinister proportions was created to block understanding between Christians and Jews. But this demon is extraneous; nothing in Christianity requires such a heartless view of Judaism. Is it heretical for Christians to assume that noble rather than base motives lay at the core of the Jewish unwillingness to enter the apostolic church? One does not have to idealize first-century Judaism in order to make this assertion.[31]

27. Romans, 10:1.
28. Stendahl, *op. cit.,* p. 452.
29. Amos N. Wilder, "The World Council of Churches and Judaism," *Judaism and the Christian Seminary Curriculum,* J. Bruce Long (editor), Chicago, 1966, pp. 74–75.
See also Wilder's article, "The Church and Israel in the Light of Election," *Studia Evangelica* (Vol. IV, ed. by F. L. Cross, 1968), pps. 347–357.
30. See Arthur Cohen's review of the Catholic publication, *The Bridge,* in *Judaism* (Vol. 6/no. 4/1957), p. 376.
31. Heschel, for example, declares:
"Do not the sharp divisions from Jewish tradition on the part of the early Christians who were Jews indicate some failure of communication within the spiritual climate of first century Judaism?" *Op. cit.,* p. 8.

Why cannot Christians acknowledge that Israel's disbelief after (as well as before) the resurrection was an honest disbelief, inspired not by rebellion against God, but, contrariwise, by a fervent loyalty to its covenantal vocation? Certainly, the rabbinic evidence of the first century supports this contention. Against the Christian accusation that God had punished the Jews for their rejection of Christ in the fate of Judaea (70 A.D.), the early rabbis reasserted both the continuing validity of Israel's filial relationship and their own commitment to its preservation.[32] Even in the midst of the most terrible disaster, they believed, God would not cast off the people of his choice. For Christians to speak of spiritual disobedience at a time when the faith of Judaism was actually in the process of a remarkable rebirth is, in itself, a case of blind insensitivity. One may, perhaps, excuse the apostolic church, which was caught in the throes of an impassioned religious conflict, but, as far as modern Christendom is concerned, the excuse of historical circumstances will no longer suffice. A few Christians discerned this fact at an early stage in the present theological re-evaluation. Many years ago, for example, Eugen Rosenstock-Huessy was able to say, somewhat optimistically at the time, that "the hardness of heart of the Jews is today no longer a Christian dogma."[33] Rosenstock-Huessy wrote these words before anyone dreamed of the possibility of an Auschwitz. After Auschwitz, the urgency they convey is intensified a thousand times.

Some more recent Christian writers have reinforced the same insight. Thus, Amos Wilder considers that: "No doubt those Jews who believed in the Gospel saw in Christ the Amen and the fulfillment of all the promises of God, as Christians do today. But Israel as a whole in faithfulness to God's covenant as

32. See Benjamin W. Helfgott, *The Doctrine of Election in Tannaitic Literature,* New York, 1954, especially chapters I–IV.
33. *Briefe,* p. 696. Cited by Schoeps, *op. cit.,* p. 145.

they understood it could not agree, and they have continued in their faithfulness to this day."[34]

To Eckardt, "the Israel of Jesus' day, and the Israel which lives upon Torah in any day, not only bears no real moral liability for the alleged non-acceptance of Jesus, but is, on the contrary, to be praised for undeviating fealty to its recognition of the divine promises."[35]

Perhaps it is appropriate to cite a great modern Jewish theologian as well. "It is arrogant to maintain that the Jews' refusal to accept Jesus as the Messiah is due to their stubbornness or blindness as it would be presumptuous for the Jews not to acknowledge the glory and holiness in the lives of countless Christians."[36]

When this demon dies, the real dialogue will begin. A further question, however, remains to be answered. Even with the healing of time that Schwarzschild desires, can Judaism and Christianity, so closely akin and yet so sharply divided in certain fundamental matters, find a basis for mutual tolerance and mutual love despite their conflicting interpretations of the Hebrew scriptures and the divine self-revelation in history? It seems to me that they can. According to what appears to be a popular Jewish view, expressed, for example, by Arthur Cohen, Christianity is a well-intentioned mistake to be corrected by God at the end of time.[37] Cohen, like Buber, believes that the messianic age has not yet dawned, so that man awaits in exile his promised deliverance.[38] Christians, in Jewish eyes, are wrong in affirming

34. Wilder, *op. cit.*, pps. 74–75.
35. Eckardt, "Can There Be a Jewish-Christian Relationship?" *op. cit.* p. 129.
36. Abraham Heschel, "No Religion Is an Island," *Union Seminary Quarterly Review* (Vol. XXI/no. 2, part 1/January 1966), p. 129.
37. Cohen, *op. cit.*
38. See Cohen's book, *The Natural and the Supernatural Jew*, New York, 1962.
Cohen uses the idea of "exile" as a basis for a theology of Jewish existence.

that redemption has visited the earth in a decisive fashion, but at least their error is well meant.

If religious Jews are capable of regarding Christianity in such a spirit of magnanimity, surely the least that Christians can do is to respond in the same spirit. Instead of viewing the Jewish failure to accept Jesus as a tragic act of disobedience premised on a quasi-Pauline "mystery," or hardness of heart, the church might well regard this failure as nothing worse than a well-intentioned mistake born out of a profound rabbinical allegiance to the same God whom Christians worship as the Father of Jesus Christ. The ultimate question as to whether historic Judaism or historic Christianity is right in its confessional stance must remain insoluble in time, but, as Cohen suggests, it can safely be left for God to resolve at the end of time. In the meantime, each faith has its own distinctive witness to bear.

There is no valid reason why Christian theology cannot take this step. It does not require the renunciation of a single genuine Christian tenet. Dialogue, thus liberated from a great weight of unnecessary encumbrances, may, when time has cured all wounds and terminated all silences, eventually take form and substance as a living bond between the church and the synagogue. Then, in a way more authentic and less contrived than the schism theologians prescribe, the Jews will indeed become part of an ecumenical movement larger and more flexible than its present reality. They will never become members of the Christian *oikoumene* in a concrete organic sense, but, in a larger ecumenical sense, their relationship with the church will always reflect a special status that no other religious community of mankind can ever claim.

IX. Anti-Semitism and the Shape of Things to Come

If it has become a theological commonplace to speak of the future of Jewish-Christian relations in terms of dialogue, it has also become a theological commonplace to portray the future of the post-Constantinian church in terms of the old Jewish condition of diaspora. Christians, it is alleged, await the same fate in society that Jews have endured for centuries. The number of prophetic voices who have seized upon this historical analogy has been increasing in recent years. Perhaps Johannes Hoekendijk is a representative example: "If no unexpected changes occur in the world of tomorrow, the churches will find themselves again clearly in a *diaspora* situation: living in dispersion as thinly spread minority groups. . . . Together we are pushed to the fringe of society in order there to serve as a 'proportionally ever decreasing minority.' There we shall encounter one another as people who have left their fortified positions and now only vaguely remember those strong and solid houses which they once inhabited—or we shall not meet one another at all; there, on the fringe, we shall recognize each other as 'Hebrews'—or we shall not recognize one another at all."[1]

1. J. C. Hoekendijk, *The Church Inside Out,* trans. by Isaac C. Rottenberg, Philadelphia, 1964, pps. 186–187.

Whether or not this somewhat pessimistic vision of the Christian future will prove exactly true, there is no doubt that the comfortable period of ascendancy that the church has enjoyed in most western nations is drawing to a close. Already, in Marxist territories, it has ended. Although, generally speaking, the shape of the future has some ominous implications for institutional Christianity, in one respect at least it bears the signs of hope. For the first time since the earliest Christian centuries, Christians and Jews are beginning to confront each other with an approximate degree of cultural equality. This, in itself, is likely to prove a continued stimulus toward reform as far as the church is concerned, unless the latter should harden its intellectual and emotional defenses. There is even an exciting quality in the new historical juxtaposition. Suddenly, as Hoekendijk declares, Christians, living in an unaccustomed environment, may learn to think of themselves as "Hebrews" again, as they re-experience the Abrahamic adventure. The church, moreover, in assuming the charactor of an "Exodus Church,"[2] may acquire a new affinity with the original people of the exile, whose long insecure pilgrimage throughout western history has not really ceased with the partial security afforded to a minority of Jews by the modern state of Israel. A diaspora shared together should prove a fertile breeding ground of mutual understanding as time proceeds. In this respect, the future is bright rather than dark, despite the fact that, at present, the dialogue falters owing to the temporal proximity of Auschwitz and the unsettled account of Christian complicity.

At least as critical as the future of the church is the future of anti-semitism. What lies in store for civilization after Auschwitz? Is optimism or pessimism the appropriate mood as the twentieth century lurches into its final decades? Will anti-semitism, as the

2. Juergen Moltmann, *Theology of Hope, On the Ground and Implications of a Christian Eschatology,* trans. by James W. Leitch, New York, 1965, chapter V.

optimists believe, wither away during the emergence of a new political, social and economic ethos in a world in the throes of rapid change? Or, as the pessimists believe, will anti-semitism persist in different and unimagined forms, perhaps to ravage the earth again in some new holocaust?

One famous optimist was Sartre. Writing in 1948, during his intellectual flirtation with the far left, Sartre ventured this bold dictum: "What is there to say except that the socialist revolution is necessary to and sufficient for the suppression of the anti-Semite? It is for the Jews also that we shall make the revolution."[3] Although anti-semitism thrives in the corrupt atmosphere of a bourgeois society, in other words, it could not survive for long if forced to inhale the pure air of a just society.

Curiously reminiscent of Sartre's optimism is a much more recent prophesy uttered by an American Jewish historian, Ellis Rivkin. Rivkin's premises, however, are the reverse of Sartre's faith in socialism. Not global communism or socialism, but global capitalism will dissolve anti-semitism as a significant threat to the Jewish community, as the social order of the future impinges upon the present age. The character of the post-Auschwitz world is revealing itself increasingly as that of a developing global community dominated by an unprecedented economic expansionism. Anti-semitism, on the other hand, has, in Rivkin's view, always required economic stagnation and bad times in order to capture the masses. It is only logical, therefore, to expect its virtual disappearance now that the "age of the nation state is nearing its end, and the era of permanent and sustained economic growth is being ushered in."[4] With this new era, "the monstrous extermination policies of the Nazis will fade as a transient experiment with barbarism."[5] Jews, Rivkin feels, can

3. Sartre, *op. cit.,* pps. 150–151.
4. Ellis Rivkin, "The Jew in American Society," *The Central Conference of American Rabbis Yearbook* (Vol. LXXVII/1967), p. 216.
5. *Ibid.,* p. 215.

175

survey the future with optimism, since the current of modern history is flowing in a favorable direction. Only if this current should unexpectedly alter its course will the danger exist again.

But Sartre's optimism has already been refuted by the turn of events, and Rivkin's optimism may suffer the same fate. Certainly, a reading of the available evidence does not encourage the notion that anti-semitism is a waning peril, especially in the Soviet Union and in some of the Latin American nations.[6] One need not be a believer in the various religious theories of "eternal anti-semitism" in order to suspect the presence of the anti-semite for a long time to come. The predictions of Sartre and Rivkin assume that the particular, and quite different explanations of anti-semitism implicit in their respective writings are definitive. But, as we stated in the first chapter, anti-semitism has many facets which do not easily lend themselves to simplistic and self-confident explanations of any description. Rivkin's globalist views, moreover, are open to question as well.

If the international Jewish community would be foolhardy in considering itself immune to future dangers, then even less can the post-Auschwitz church afford the luxury of a complacent prognosis. A church that played an indirect role in the making of Auschwitz in the first place, and, following this event, has not fully repented of its sins, has a special stake in the prevention of new Auschwitzs whenever they threaten. Even the relatively mild, genteel anti-semitism of American society cannot be regarded casually. This level of anti-semitism, diagnosed effectively by E. Digby Baltzell,[7] concentrates on the exclusion of Jews from country clubs, university administrations and the higher echelons of the business world, and is especially insidious because it wears the mantle of respectability. But the worship

6. See, for example, the publication *Current Anti-Semitic Activities Abroad, A Survey*, The American Jewish Committee, Institute of Human Relations, New York, 1963.

7. E. Digby Baltzell, *The Protestant Establishment, Aristocracy and Caste in America*, Random House, New York, 1964.

of caste is not far removed from the worship of race; both are forms of a common idolatry, and differ in degree rather than essence. Protestant Christianity, moreover, seems, for historic reasons, especially susceptible to the lures of caste prejudice in the Anglo-Saxon nations: after all, the "P" in "WASP" is for Protestant, and the significance of this term in America is not minor. Thus, a special moral duty rests on conscientious Protestants to liberate their churches from the kind of natural connection with the "Protestant Establishment" (Baltzell), and its polite anti-semitism, which it so readily fosters. The Negro revolution in America does not provide the only urgent moral impetus for this step.

In the second chapter, we dwelt upon the need for a revitalized Christian conscience able to function with much greater power in the world than the enfeebled conscience of the German church prior to Auschwitz. Only if the conscience of the church is reborn will the guilt of Auschwitz begin the process of expiation, and Christians find restoration to a better spiritual health. This statement must now be enlarged. As a necessary ingredient in its rebirth, the conscience of modern Christianity requires, I believe, the acceptance of a special Christian responsibility toward the Jewish world: a responsibility both to oppose anti-semitism whenever and wherever it manifests itself, and to assist by every human means its past, present and future victims. Here, I am adopting Thieme's idea of a new Christian diaconate to the church's separated "older brother,"[8] only based on the exigencies of the twentieth century. This, surely, is one of the more creative and concrete suggestions to emerge in recent theology on the subject of Jew and Christian in their mutual interaction. Such a diaconate would have the advantage of great practicality and, in the best sense, a supreme theological relevance to the situation. It is, in addition, thoroughly sound in its historic and religious origins, reviving an ancient form of minis-

8. Chapter V.

try in a modern setting. If sponsored by a church also in a state of diaspora, it could prove the means of inspiring a measure of the radical faith which characterized the primitive Christian community. The early Christians did not require the sanction and protection of a *societas Christiana* in order to obey the love commandment. But modern Christians have fed too long on more cautious instincts. They need a radicalized spirit. A love that accepts an element of personal risk for the sake of the neighbor cannot be enacted without transforming something integral to the religious being of anyone who exhibits this kind of daring.

An opportunity tragically missed for such a demonstration of brotherly help was the Arab-Israeli War in the summer of 1967. As a case-study of what remains wrong in Jewish-Christian relations, this episode is highly instructive. Jews and Christians (with a few notable exceptions in the latter community) did not in the least see the issues in a similar fashion. Most Christians, for example, revealed a shocking inability to appreciate the universal Jewish fear of a second Auschwitz: a fact, as Emil Fackenheim has pointed out, that in itself becomes a revelation of how profoundly the churches have failed to understand the true implications of the first Auschwitz.[9] The tendency among Christian commentators was rather to view the struggle in political terms alone, and to choose sides accordingly. Some, on the basis of a fundamentalist interpretation of the prophetic literature of the Old Testament, sided with Israel (for example, Dr. Billy Graham). Others expressed a degree of sympathy with the Arab nations, several of which contain important Christian minorities.

9. "If in May 1967 the Christian community did not cry out against a second Auschwitz, it was not because of its indifference to the words emanating from Cairo and Damascus, but rather because it did not hear them. It failed to recognize the danger of a second Holocaust because it has yet to recognize the fact of the first."
Emil L. Fackenheim, "Jewish Faith and the Holocaust: a Fragment," *Commentary* (Vol. 46/no. 2/August, 1968), p. 35.

Whether pro-Arab or pro-Israeli, however, few Christians were sufficiently imaginative to perceive the meaning of Israel to the average Jew, not to mention the instinctive connection that Jews everywhere made between the latest threat of liquidation and the holocaust of an earlier decade in the same country. Regrettably, some Christians, seemingly under the spell of Arnold Toynbee, chose to pass moral judgment on Zionism for creating a Jewish state in the first place.[10] In taking this position, they overlooked the fact that the Zionist movement was conceived largely, if not exclusively, as a Jewish response to western anti-semitism in the nineteenth century,[11] so that, in an indirect manner, Israel is the child of "Christian" prejudice. Yet these Christians were genuinely surprised and personally hurt when the Jewish-Christian dialogue suffered a near-fatal setback as a result of their non-committal stance. Few, thus far, have assimilated the depths of the disillusionment experienced by dialogue-minded Jews after the affair reached its dénouement.

Because the breakdown in communication was so serious, it is necessary to probe its causes more closely. While Eckardt is undoubtedly right in diagnosing the presence of a more substantial dose of gentile anti-semitism in the attitude of Christians than the official responses (or non-responses) of their churches to the crisis would indicate,[12] he probably goes too far when he implies that the majority of Christian believers were secretly hoping for an Arab victory. "Once the Assyrians were the rod of God's anger: today, there is a man by the name of Nasser. We wonder . . . After all, the Arab people have never *really* rejected Christ. Could not they be instruments of divine judgment upon Israel?"[13] The truth, rather, is that the Christian

10. See, for example, the various articles by A. C. Forrest in *The United Church Observer*, such as "What Happened when I Criticized Israel" (Vol. 138/no. 10/April 1, 1968), pps. 27f.

11. Documented in Hertzberg, *The Zionist Idea,* and elsewhere.

12. Eckardt, "Again, Silence in the Churches," *op. cit.*, pps. 163–177.

13. *Ibid.*, pps. 171-172.

community has never understood that Israel, as far as Jews are concerned, is a symbol in some sense analogous to the Christian symbol of resurrection: after death (Auschwitz), God miraculously raised his people to life (Israel) in the midst of the nations. To non-religious Jews, to be sure, the miracle is a secular miracle, but nonetheless real and potent in the Jewish consciousness. Since Christians, as our whole study has emphasized, have been slow in grasping the ramifications of Auschwitz after a period of more than twenty years, their inability to grasp the existential dimensions of the Jewish plight in 1967— and later, in face of this miracle—is merely additional evidence of how apart the church has drifted from its closest spiritual relative. It is this fact, in the last analysis, that is most shocking.

Toynbee himself can be interpreted most charitably as a symptom of this general alienation. He acknowledges quite freely his innate lack of sympathy with Judaism as a religion, regarding it as a source of fanaticism because of the divisions that the concept of a chosen people breeds in the human community.[14] Seeing no great value in the Jewish self-identity either in religious terms or as a people, he transfers his antipathy to Zionism and its creation, Israel. The latter, for Toynbee, should never have been permitted to be born, because of the greater claim to the Palestinian soil of the indigenous Arab population, much of which now exists in a refugee state. But Toynbee's case is weak historically,[15] and totally ignores the critical point that, while a return to Eretz Israel has been a part of Jewish religious longing since the catastrophe of 70 A.D.,

14. Anti-Judaism is a fairly consistent theme in most of Toynbee's writings, emerging with special clarity in *A Historian's Approach to Religion.*

15. See the debate between Toynbee and Solomon Zeitlin, "Jewish rights in Palestine," "Jewish rights in Eretz Israel (Palestine)," *The Jewish Quarterly Review* (Vol. LII/nos. 1, 4), 1962.

Zeitlin is no match for Toynbee on the stylistic level, and his argument suffers from too much polemic of an emotional nature. Nevertheless, it seems to me that he makes the stronger case.

180

the failure of assimilation and the bitter wells of modern anti-semitism made the Zionist movement an inevitability. Morally speaking, the least that the western nations owed the Jewish people—especially after Auschwitz—was some form of Zionist solution. No other solution was even faintly realistic (certainly not the one suggested by Toynbee himself[16]), and, given the profound and legitimate attachment to the soil of Palestine which has never been surrendered by Jews at any time, none could have satisfied their aspirations more fully. Toynbee, however, recognizes only one moral issue in the matter: the rights of the Palestinian Arabs. But Israel's claim is also moral.

To say this, of course, is not to blind oneself to the human problems of the Jewish resettlement, especially the pathetic situation of the displaced Arabs, although the responsibility for the latter is probably much less Israeli than Toynbee asserts. Nor, in calling for a Christian diaconate toward the Jews, does it follow that Israel, as a nation-state, is to be considered above reproach. Like every other nation-state, Israel is subject to moral ambiguities, and neither Christian nor Jew is justified in assigning *carte-blanche* appproval to every Israeli policy—particularly its recent expansionist tendencies. But such a diaconate must involve an acknowledgment on the part of Christians of Israel's intrinsic right to exist; that is the point at which I part company with those Christians who cite Toynbee as their authority. Otherwise, a diaconate is not possible at all; indeed, it becomes a mockery. For this reason, the summer of 1967 was an opportunity missed. ". . . I have wondered passingly," writes Sandmel, "how the neutral Christians would have felt if Israel had been defeated instead of being victorious, and if the two million Jews there had been annihilated."[17] No doubt, the churches would have been greatly shocked, but the tragedy would have been accomplished. Christians should have spoken, for even the de-

16. *Ibid.,* p. 7.
17. Sandmel, *op. cit.,* p. 55.

struction of the state of Israel, not to mention its inhabitants, would have been a disaster; the world needs Israel, both as a reminder of past western anti-semitism and as a rebuke to future anti-semites. It also needs Israel as a continuing refuge for Jews who may yet be victimized in other parts of the globe.

Apart from the question of Israel, and the never-ending need of Jews for support in the face of anti-semitism (including its fashionable contemporary guise of anti-Zionism), the diaconate, as we have stressed, is a necessity for the church's own inner well-being. Christian ethics has a few lessons to learn from the Nazi rape of the German conscience, and one lesson is the danger of identifying too intimately the culture of a given time and place with the interests of Christian civilization. For the mere fact of possessing a Christian tradition guarantees nothing, and no religious commitment is immune to the inroads of human idolatry in the form of cultural ideologies. A "Christian" nation is, at best, a misnomer, and, at worst (as Germany illustrates), an invitation for an uncritical worship of the power lusts and imperialisms that infect every age. This lesson, however, has trouble making itself remembered, and, in order to be effective, requires a strong counter-prevailing tug of conscience pulling the Christian community against the currents of contemporary culture which so easily carry religious majorities downstream. The Jews, always a minority and seldom participants in superpatriotic enthusiasms in any nation, warn the church, as Tillich declares, not to barter the "Lord of time" for the "gods of space." The more closely Christians serve their Jewish neighbors in the spirit of Christian *diakonia*, thereby identifying with them, the more likely they are to heed this warning.

Germany, to be sure, was an extreme case. Beginning with Luther, whose doctrine of the two realms produced an absolute division between the inward authority of religion and the outward authority of secular rule, German Protestantism had long been conditioned to attitudes of subservience toward the state. No tradition of social criticism ever succeeded in establishing itself within the framework of pre-Auschwitz Lutheran ethics. Illustrations of the German Protestant obsession with civic obedience are legion, but nowhere does this trait appear more tragically than in the theological reflections of Dietrich Bonhoeffer, whose fragmentary *Ethics* was actually composed during the author's personal struggle against the Nazi tyranny. In spite of everything that he faced personally, Bonhoeffer could not emancipate himself from a conservative Lutheran mentality. "The claim of government, which is based on its power and its mission, is the claim of God and is binding upon conscience. . . . In the exercise of the mission of government the demand for obedience is unconditional and qualitatively total; it extends both to conscience and to bodily life. Belief, conscience and bodily life are subject to an obligation of obedience with respect to the divine commission of government."[18] While Bonhoeffer does allow for civic disobedience in extreme cases, should a government offend the divine commandment (which Nazism clearly did), his qualification, in true Lutheran fashion, is tiny indeed. "The Christian is neither obliged nor able to examine the rightfulness of the demand of government in each particular case. . . . In cases of doubt, obedience is required; for the Christian does not bear the responsibility of government."[19]

It is incredible, in retrospect, to think that Bonhoeffer—an opponent of Hitler with all his heart—could have believed this doctrine. The fact, however, that he did makes it somewhat easier to understand the nonchalance with which the majority of German Christians initially accepted Nazi rule. Hitler, in addition, acquired office by legal means, and could claim

18. Bonhoeffer, *Ethics,* trans. by Neville Norton Smith, New York, 1955, pps. 306–307.
19. *Ibid.*

legitimacy for his chancellorship before the trappings of democracy, having served their purpose, were cast aside. The German churches thus did not, until it was too late, see him as a tyrant whose reign was destined to offend the commandment of God. Had they been more perceptive earlier, the *Theological Declaration of Barmen* (1934), written by Barth as a creed for the Christian opposition, might have departed more radically from the two-realms idea in its definition of the church-state relationship;[20] not even Barth, however, grasped the true need of the hour as far as traditional ethics were concerned. Today, as a consequence of Auschwitz, Lutheran theologians are engaged in a sharp critique of their tradition, but the lesson should have been learned prior to Auschwitz. The combination of an authoritarian political ethic and a corrupted theological image of Judaism was sufficient, apart from any secular forces, to render much of the religious conscience of German Christianity supine before a rising anti-semitic totalitarianism. For Hitler, the church situation was perfect.

Fortunately, outside of its Lutheran version, the Christian faith has always possessed other resources of wisdom with which to fashion a social ethic, notably the libertarian heritage of the radical Protestant sects of the seventeenth century.[21] (The Anabaptist movement, significantly, was not successful in its efforts to radicalize the political ethic of the German Reformation.) Thus, an unquestioning acceptance of secular power structures is not characteristic of the western churches today. Even in the most traditionalist societies, such as Spain, the signs of Christian social unrest are becoming apparent. The more the church as a whole turns to a diaspora existence, the sharper its

20. Trans. in Arthur C. Cochrane, *The Church's Confession Under Hitler,* Philadelphia, 1962, pps. 237–242.
    The state, in this Declaration, still owes its authority to divine appointment.
21. That is, the puritan sects of the Cromwellian revolution in England.

sense of differentiation from the vested interests of social ruling classes is bound to become. Under the pressure of the many revolutionary ferments that are convulsing the western nations today, the tendency among Christian theologians is to proclaim a new freedom of ethical decision, liberating the Christian citizen from ecclesiastical doctrines which, whether Catholic or Protestant, emphasize the moral duty of obedience to rulers presumably appointed by God (Romans 13). That notion was the curse of German Christianity. But it is plainly impossible to regard the Hitlers of the world as divine appointees! Nor is it possible to regard order as intrinsically more meritorious than justice, as the conservatives of every generation always believe. Order and justice exist in tension, and anarchy is no worse an evil than the cannibalistic order of the totalitarian state. Auschwitz, at least, has clarified that truth.

A Christian diaconate toward the Jews, therefore, in addition to being concerned about the fate of the state of Israel, requires a radicalization of Christian political ethics wherever authoritarian doctrines still prevail. Anything that is capable of crippling moral resistance against state policies of anti-semitism reveals its inadequacy as a guide for Christian living in the context of the modern world. Although pre-Auschwitz Germany presented an unusually sick combination of factors, post-war democratic societies should not congratulate themselves on the inviolability of their institutions in the face of anti-democratic challenges. One only has to sample the literature of the radical right in America in order to discover how tenuous these institutions are; here, for example, the concept of a "Christian" nation still finds popularity, and anti-semitism is nourished as an instrument of right-wing politics.[22] At best, the shape of the future is highly uncertain, and sensitive Christians know that the church cannot afford any new flirtations with incipient anti-

22. See Benjamin R. Epstein and Arnold Foster, *The Radical Right, Report on the John Birch Society and Its Allies,* New York, 1967.

semitic political parties. Because the measure of anti-semitism to which a society is prone remains one crucial index of its moral health, the measure to which the Christian community is willing to make the struggle of the Jews its own struggle remains an index to both its own spiritual fibre and the Christian capacity to meet the other moral testings of the age.

The diaconate also has another aspect which should not be urged lightly. If Christians wish to serve Jews in a brotherly spirit, they must, as we have suggested, swallow their traditional reflexes, and abandon all forms of religious proselytism, including the subtle use of dialogue as an opportunity to make converts. Although, as Peter Schneider and others have pointed out, some exceptional Christians who specialized in missions to the Jews in the past were also vigorous opponents of racialist anti-semitism,[23] the fact cannot be gainsaid that, in Christian history, conversionism and anti-Judaism have been frequent bedfellows. Too much theological prejudice was incorporated into Christian piety for too long a period to effect an easy separation in the twentieth century. Unless Christians restrain their evangelistic zeal toward the Jewish people, it is doubtful if a complete separation will ever occur. (The argument that the church also shows an anti-semitic face in *refusing* to proselytize Jews is not convincing. This is one area in which the latter are likely to welcome discrimination. A church is only anti-semitic if its members should refuse to receive a Jewish applicant for membership on the ground of his Jewish identity: a different thing entirely.) There is, moreover, a deeper reason for regarding missions to the Jews as incompatible with the kind of Christian moral duty embodied in the diaconate idea.

This reason is simple, and has been expressed by theologians as diverse as Parkes and Barth: the Jews are in reality a special case. "When Paul sought to be a Jew to Jews, it was not just

23. Peter Schneider, *The Dialogue of Christians and Jews*, New York, 1966, p. 159.

formally but materially *toto caelo* different from when he sought to be a Greek to the Greeks."[24] One does not have to accept Barth's peculiar doctrine of the synagogue in order to agree with his judgment at this juncture. Christians, who learned of the God of biblical monotheism from the lips of Hebrew priests and Hebrew prophets, certainly have nothing to teach the spiritual descendants of ancient Israel in this essential respect. Had, as the church claimed, the religious pulse of rabbinic Judaism really ceased to beat throughout the Christian centuries, causing all knowledge of God to ebb out of the life of the Jewish community, the matter might have assumed a different character today. But, in spite of the many phases and transformations through which Judaism has passed, and the variety of religious styles among modern Jews, Christians cannot fairly make this claim. Although his existence has been feeble at times, the "supernatural Jew" (Cohen), like the "supernatural Christian," is still a reality. It is this Jew to whom the Christian must relate in a manner *toto caelo* different than to other men.

What, in that case, remains of the universal imperative of the gospel, that is, the missionary injunction to "baptize all nations"?[25] Must the church repudiate these time-honored words attributed by the early church to the risen Christ? (One can, of course, always dispose of this Matthaean verse by dismissing it as an ecclesiastical appendage. But it reflects the mind of primitive Christianity, if not the mind of Jesus himself.) At first glance, this would seem to be the case, if the Jews are excepted from the nations ("*ethne*"), but such a conclusion does not follow automatically. It can only be made to follow if one assumes that the goal of Christian faith is literally to cover the earth with Christian converts, thereby making Christianity the sole religion of mankind. The nonsense of this position, how-

24. Barth, *CD*, Vol. IV/3/2, p. 877, fn.
25. Matthew, 28:19–20.

ever, is apparent to a moment's reflection. Is the meaning of mission primarily, or even secondarily, a numerical one? There is no evidence that the church of the first century ever set itself such an improbable task; the parousia, for one thing, was expected well in advance of any mass Christianization of the known (and much smaller) world in which Christianity was born. Also, as W. Cantwell Smith has pointed out, the ancients never thought in terms of "religions" in any case: the division of men into religious groupings is a basically modern method of categorization.[26] To the apostolic church, Judaism was not another religion, nor were the mystery cults of Hellenism and the Roman world. Hence, if the idea of mission is probed, something more profound is at stake than a recruitment campaign designed to swallow the entire population of the earth into the church.

The meaning of mission is another side of the meaning of discipleship. The quality of Christian discipleship is always a more authentic measure of the seriousness of the church's faith than the number of converts that can be added to ecclesiastical statistics in any age. How many converts did Jesus make, or seek to make? But the path of redemptive suffering which constituted the core of his messiahship was a matter with a different priority. Jesus was unconcerned with converting people to a religion, but deeply concerned with serving them through his personal enactment of the role of a servant. His ministry provides the church with its true pattern of mission.

There is also another consideration. The era of the New Testament was an era which required a rapid expansionism, especially the inclusion of the Gentiles within the boundaries of the people of God. This was the basis of Paul's apostleship. In one way or another, Christianity has continued to expand throughout its history, and the process has not come to a halt in the twentieth century. The swift penetration of the modern

26. W. Cantwell Smith, *The Meaning and End of Religion,* New York, 1963.

church into some parts of Africa and Asia represents an extension of the same impulse which drove Paul on his original apostolic journeys. Nonetheless, it can be questioned as to whether simple expansionism is the dominant need of Christianity in the present era. Or does God attach more importance to other matters? That is the relevant theological issue.

Recently, Edward Schillebeeckx has insisted that the best Christian posture in a post-Christian era (meaning the western world after the disappearance of Christendom, where most Jews dwell) is not the proselytizing of non-Christians, but the living of life in the distinctive New Testament style of *agapé*. In the first place, according to Schillebeeckx, the non-Christian segment of humanity already belongs to Christ in a larger sense: "The Church is actively present even where her adequate ecclesial form has not yet appeared. The contrast between the Church and mankind cannot be equated with an opposition between Church and non-Church."[27] In the second place, serving humanity in an agapistic spirit is in itself a genuine apostolic venture, not a dilution of Christian responsibility in the light of Christ's commission: "In the Church's confrontation with mankind in history her members must be living examples and 'types' of this overflowing love and manifest their willingness to give up their personal lives in the service of others."[28] One has only to go a step further and add that, as far as the Jews are concerned, this kind of apostolic relationship has a special pertinence.

Schillebeeckx is not the only theologian to interpret mission in this vain. Much earlier, Bonhoeffer originated the notion of the church forming itself "in conformity with the form of Christ,"[29] that is to say, manifesting in its collective life (as well as the individual lives of believers) the pattern of suffering, death and resurrection that emerges from the career of Jesus

27. Edward Schillebeeckx, "The Church and Mankind," *The Church and Mankind*, Dogma, Vol. I, Glen Rock, 1964, p. 87.
28. *Ibid.*, p. 98.
29. Bonhoeffer, *op. cit.*, p. 21.

himself. Figuratively, in other words, the Christian community should assume a christological shape in the world. While Bonhoeffer, strictly speaking, cannot be described as a martyr on behalf of the Jews, a few German Christians apparently joined the death march for almost no other reason.[30] Can there be any question but that their diaconate was christological in a far truer sense than the attitude of Christians who combined, as many did, a concern for Jewish souls with an indifference toward their bodies?

Throughout these pages, we have sought to examine the theology of the church concerning the Jews from the perspective of anti-semitism. The perspective is important, for almost anything has a different character depending upon the angle of vision that the viewer adopts. Had Auschwitz never occurred, and had Christendom never stained its hands in the sordid tale of anti-semitism, Christian theology would not have come under such heavy censure. Certain ideas might now be regarded as foolish or quaint, but scarcely as demonic. Jews might well have laughed at the idea that their history stands under a curse, except that the joke did not prove funny. Auschwitz had altered the criteria of theology forever. The beliefs and doctrines of Christianity must be weighed not solely for their inner logic, but immeasurably more for their human ramifications. Never again, one trusts, will the church dogmatize abstractly about human themes without pre-testing its conclusions in the crucible of the flesh-and-blood world with its manifold possibilities of cruelty. All excuse for theological innocence has ended.

Only in the afternoon of the twentieth century, after its terrible midday, have Christians begun to absorb this lesson in its most sober dimensions. No Jew is likely to forget Auschwitz. No Christian can afford to blot its horror from his memory, for theology, like history, has changed its character, and nothing can reverse the situation.

30. For example, Provost Bernhard Lichtenberg.

Index